P9-CMF-967

PROPHETS OF THE SOUL

PROPHETS OF THE SOUL

JOSEPH M. M. GRAY

"I like a prophet of the soul."—*Emerson*

Essay Index Reprint Series

BOOKS FOR LIBRARIES PRESS
FREEPORT, NEW YORK

First Published 1936
Reprinted 1971

INTERNATIONAL STANDARD BOOK NUMBER:
0-8369-2277-8

LIBRARY OF CONGRESS CATALOG CARD NUMBER:
71-156655

PRINTED IN THE UNITED STATES OF AMERICA

CONTENTS

FOREWORD

THE biographical chapters herewith presented are not intended to be complete either as delineations of character or expositions of theology. But two aspects of the contemporary scene would appear to excuse the publication of the volume. The first is that this generation does not hold the pulpit in the high esteem with which in other times it was regarded. This is not simply because religion has come to be too much considered merely one of the enterprises of life, an option rather than, as formerly, the inescapable imperative; but also because other agencies of information and intellectual stimulus seem now to be more vital and reliable, and more vitally and reliably related to the actual world. The second aspect of contemporary life is that of the conflict between those who want religion more "liberalized" and those who, disillusioned by the apparent bankruptcy of liberalism in politics and theology alike, would carry it back to an extremely conservative theology which, while not openly avowing Calvinism, involves conceptions of Necessity no less fatal to spiritual recovery because concealed under impassioned, to say nothing of cryptic, phrases.

I have wanted, therefore, to show, even though it should be done only far too sketchily, the part taken by preachers, as such, in the progress of liberal thought in American Protestantism. My hope has been not only that some renewal of respect for the pulpit may be born in those who read this volume, but also that the younger preachers shall regain that sense of the primacy of preaching which will recall them from the various preoccupations they have substituted for devotion to the prophetic pulpit. Only such devotion will justify their vocation in a society which turns to the precisions of the expert for its scientific and social information, but religiously is pretty well content with echoes of its fathers' faith heard faintly from a disregarded past.

The book lists follow the chapters not to give the volume an air of erudition which it does not deserve but to suggest to any readers who may desire them sources of much ampler knowledge of the men and their periods than the chapters offer. For counsel and suggestions in respect of the lists I am indebted to my colleague, Professor Wesley M. Gewehr, whose volume on *The Great Awakening in Virginia* could not be omitted from any bibliography of the subject. My thanks are also due to Bishop William F. McDowell for helpful criticism of the manuscript; to the ministers in many summer schools, whose reception of some of the lectures which were the basis of the volume encouraged its publication; and to an unusual degree to Dr. Allan MacRossie for his stimulating interest both in the lectures and in the book, and for a personal friendship which has enriched many years.

J. M. M. G.

The American University

I

THOSE MATHERS AND THE PURITAN COMMONWEALTH

I

THOSE MATHERS AND THE PURITAN COMMONWEALTH

THERE were three of those Mathers, Richard, Increase, and Cotton, and for us the line begins with Richard. He was born in England in 1596 and had education enough when he was fifteen years old to be the schoolmaster in a village near Liverpool. Here, when he was eighteen, he was converted, and shortly afterward went to Oxford, returning in 1618 to the village where he had been the schoolmaster, but now to be its minister in the Established Church. The *Mayflower* was not to sail for two years yet, but conformity was a good deal more in the air and in men's convictions than our slight acquaintance with history sometimes allows us to realize; and even at the time of his ordination Richard Mather was Puritan enough to be apprehensive of the consequences. Nevertheless, it was not until he had preached for fifteen years that he was suspended for his nonconformity. The sympathetic tolerance of the orthodox Church can be seen in the remark of one of the clergy who, when he was told that Mather had not worn a surplice in all the fifteen years of his ministry, replied, in franker language than I dare use today, notwithstanding the educational efficiency of the movies and contemporary fiction, that it would have been better for him if he had been the father of seven illegitimate children.

Suspended in England, quite naturally he turned to America, arriving in Boston in 1635. Looking back across the generations which separate us, the Puritans appear to be reactionaries; so much so that the very name has long since become a synonym for bigotry, narrowness, and restraint. But no one will ever understand them until he realizes that they were actually Protestants with all that the word means, and that their exodus to America was a pilgrimage to freedom.

Within a year Richard Mather had gathered together a church in Boston, and there he lived, preached, and served some thirty-four years, dying in great pain, in 1669. A constant and laborious student, his concern to the very last was for his books. On the day before he died he persuaded some friends to help him into his study but was too weak to remain. "I see," he said, "I am not able; I have not been in my study for several days; and is it not a lamentable thing, that I should lose so much time?" When he was asked, amid his suffering, how he was, his characteristic answer was, "Far from well, yet far better than mine iniquities deserve." His first wife died in 1654, when the youngest and most famous of her seven sons was about fifteen years old; and that son is the second of these Mathers with whom this chapter deals.

He was named Increase "because," as his son in after years was to record, "of the never-to-be-forgotten *Increase,* of every sort, wherewith God favored the country, about the time of his nativity." That was the year 1639, from which time, according to his own report, he swam quietly in a stream of impiety until a serious illness started him on the way to conversion. He took his first degree at Harvard in 1656, when he was seventeen years old, arguing his thesis, so one of the examiners said, like a great scholar, and on his birthday a year later he preached his first sermon in a village of Dorchester. The next Sunday he preached in his father's pulpit. A month later he sailed to England and went from there to Dublin, where one of his brothers was a minister, and entered Trinity College, where he secured the degree of Master of Arts. He declined a Fellowship, and after preaching for a winter, became chaplain to a military garrison. The year 1660 saw the Restoration of Charles II and faced this Mather with the alternative of conformity or dissent. He sailed for home and in August arrived at his father's house, being at the time twenty-two years old. He began at once to preach, alternating in his father's church and in the "New Church," in North Boston. A preacher twenty-two years old is an easy mark for cupid, no matter how many academic degrees he has; and within seven months Increase Mather was married. A year later his first child, a son, was born; and was named Cotton.

He is the third and best known of those Mathers, and his name suggests a pleasant Puritan family monopoly. It takes us back to the Rev. John Cotton, born in Derby in 1585, who at thirteen years of age was in Trinity College, Cambridge; very early a Fellow of Emmanuel College; and at twenty-seven in spite of opposition of the Bishop, settled as minister of the famous Saint Botolph's Church in old Boston in Lincolnshire. Here as the years passed his nonconformity grew, and after twenty years he was driven out. He consulted an old clergyman as to what he should do, who told him that removing a minister was like draining a fish-pond: the good fish follow the water, but eels and other "baggage" fish stick in the mud. And John Cotton, like men before and since, came to New Boston in Massachusetts where, for nearly twenty years, he lived in the noblest fashion of a Puritan preacher until his death in 1652.

All these years he and Richard Mather had been colleagues in the gospel and the Puritan Commonwealth; and when in 1654 Richard Mather's first wife died, what should be more natural than that, shortly afterward, he should marry the widow of his friend John Cotton; which he did in 1655. With the widow came the widow's daughter Maria, and when twenty-two-year-old Increase Mather came home from England in 1661, it took less than seven months for the probable to become the actual. The son married his father's stepdaughter; and became his stepmother's son-in-law; and in time named his own son after his wife's father. So Cotton Mather comes upon the scene, and the most famous of the Puritan divines, his conflicts, egotism, devotion, and witchcraft are on the way.

I

But whatever was on the way when Cotton Mather was born, something had already arrived; that was the Puritan Commonwealth. Cotton Mather, many years afterward, in writing about his grandfather, John Cotton, said that among his other activities during his life in New-Boston he propounded unto the churches "an endeavor after a *theocracy,* as near as might be, to that which was the glory of Israel." Cromwell is a reminder that the attempt had been made in England to establish such a theocracy, into the history of which this chapter cannot go. As late as 1659 Richard Baxter's book, *A Holy Commonwealth,* supported the theory, declaring, among very many other pronouncements, that of the three ordinary forms of government, to most people and usually, democracy is the worst, and that the more "theocratical, or truly Divine, any government is, the better it is." But even before he had completed the book the swift events that were hurrying on the Restoration convinced him that he was expounding a dream already done. What failed in England need not, of necessity, be a failure in America, and in Massachusetts the Puritan Commonwealth had become a reality, transient, it is true, and from the beginning severely attacked, but in its brief day a genuine accomplishment.

Under the first charter of Massachusetts, the magistrates of the colony were elected by the freemen, the freemen being members of the Church, in 1631 compelled by law to become members. But of an estimated population of 15,000 in Massachusetts in 1643, only 1,708 were freemen. Thirty-one years later the number of freemen is put at 2,527. These figures do not represent the attendants upon church service, but only the actual members of the churches; and church membership was involved in a complex conception of three different covenants, the Covenant of Grace, the Church Covenant, and the Civil Covenant.

The Covenant of Grace, of course, was that sublime transaction within the soul by which it was assured that it was united to Christ through faith and justified by the free and incalculable grace of God. It was the direction of the will and experienced adventure of conscience by which one dared to believe himself one of the elect, as far as it was possible for a sinful creature to adventure on the benevolence of the inscrutable and, though the Puritan did not use the word, the capricious condescension of God to his salvation. Those who participated in the Covenant of Grace constituted the Church invisible, and although by their own theology, only God knew and could know who were the elect, there were several thousands of Puritans who, to all intents and purposes, were confident of their own place among the saved.

The Church Covenant was something else. The invisible Church is present wherever there is an elect saint; but the visible Church is the outward form into which the consciously elect and those consciously and devoutly desiring to be of the elect associate themselves. Therefore it was the duty of all such to join the church. "This is the *Visible Covenant,* agreement, or consent whereby they give up themselves unto the Lord, to the observing of the ordinances of Christ together in the same society, which is usually called the Church Covenant."

Those who joined the church were required to make very definite and often elaborate declarations as to their personal experience of grace. "If it be a woman, her confession made before the Elders, in private, is most usually read by the Pastor, who registered the same. . . . The man, in a solemn speech, sometimes a quarter of an hour long, shorter or longer, declareth the work of grace in his soul." The inconsistency of such positive testimony with the theory of inscrutable election, which seems so apparent to us, was evidently but little accounted in the days of the Mathers.

Theoretically, the Puritans had drawn very sharp distinction between the Covenant of Grace and the Church Covenant, between the Church invisible and the visible Church; but practically the Covenant of Grace was recognized as coinciding with the visible Church. A far greater number regularly attended the church services than actually confessed an experience of Grace and so became church members. Nevertheless, the Puritans regarded those who did not belong to the church as unregenerate no matter how regular was their attendance upon divine worship and how free from irregularity were their personal lives.

The Civil Covenant, the agreement which united them in a civil government, was wholly distinct from the others. But in practical consequences, while in theory Church and State were separated, in fact they were united originally in the theocracy for which John Cotton had argued and for the recovery of which Cotton Mather struggled all his life. Puritan literature was quite emphatic in its description of civil magistrates as independent in their duties and responsibilities, but their conduct of affairs made the magistrates little more than agents carrying out the will of the Church which was more particularly the will of the clergy.

The authority of the Bible was invoked to sanction all of this, as it has been made to sanction whatever else theocrats and others at times have greatly desired. The Puritan theology, while not deliberately shaped toward the specific purpose of re-enforcing the political regime, was very easily phrased and interpreted so as to have that effect.

> Issues which were trivial in their secular bearings became importunate and passionate because of the theological issues injected into them, and issues which would have been politically significant even in a secular society became much more so when loaded with holy passion and inflamed by religious fervor. . . . Factions and sects hence multiplied more rapidly than the population and spread like infectious fevers, so that within a few years New England was a hotbed of theological and religious dispute, and within a few decades the Holy Commonwealth exploded by the force of its own religious passion.[1]

[1] Schneider: *The Puritan Mind,* p. 52.

The most famous of those who rebelled against the Holy Commonwealth was Roger Williams, although rebellion is hardly the word to use in connection with him, for he never admitted the Holy Commonwealth's right to exist and never sought any connection with it. From the time of his arrival in New England in February, 1631, he was in violent opposition to it. A nonconforming clergyman in England, he claimed to have been driven out by Archbishop Laud, which was probably true enough; but it is also true that he had refused to participate in the forms of the Established Church, and when the pastorate of a church in New England was offered him immediately on his arriving, he refused it because it was not wholly separated from the Established Church. He refused even to join the church in Boston unless it officially renounced all connection with the English Church and publicly repented of having and professing connection with it. He demanded, also, that its members be refused permission to attend the services of an Established Church when they were visiting in England, and declined to attend even the informal meeting of the New England ministers on the ground that they were likely to develop into some form of organization that would restrict the liberty of the churches. His entire career in Massachusetts was one of increasingly obstreperous hostility to the Puritan civil government and church organization. He not only refused to join in any service, however informal, in which the prayer book was used, but he urged that no Christian should pray with any unregenerate persons even though they were of one's own blood and families. He became pastor of the church in Salem which was, apparently, after his own heart; but when the church refused to break off all association with the other churches, he left it and set up his own meeting in his home. His history does not further concern us in this chapter, but without denying his admirers' claim that he was the champion of religious liberty in America, his conception of religious liberty left something to be desired. He acknowledged no other's right of opinion, but in the beginning demanded that the churches of New England accept his judgment and from that beginning proceeded rapidly to the denial of all churches whatsoever.

Ann Hutchinson, who had been in John Cotton's church in England and followed him to America, was a member of his church in Boston. She began with opposition to the Puritan theology and eventuated in menace to the Puritan Commonwealth. The men of the Boston church were in the habit of taking notes of the Sunday sermon and then, on a weekday, gathering together to discuss them. Mrs. Hutchinson rallied the women in a similar weekly meeting to which influential men of the colony gave their support and attendance, so that, as Cotton Mather afterward wrote, "the women, like their first mother, hooked in the husbands also." Mrs. Hutchinson and her circle made sharp distinctions between "works" and "grace," to the great disparagement of the former, and with the example before them of the loose morals of the German Antinomians and the Familists in Holland, the Puritans took alarm. A long story is made short by saying that soon enough the Hutchinson group were thwarting the Puritan government in civil affairs as well as spiritual, and were brought to trial. John Cotton himself, who had been Mrs. Hutchinson's minister and had, indeed, been suspected of sharing in her views, was set to examine her. She made impossible any lesser fate than banishment when she declared boldly: "We have a new rule of practice by immediate revelations; by these we guide our conduct. Not that we expect any revelation in the way of a miracle; that is a delusion; but we despise the anathemas of your synods and courts, and will still follow the whisperings of conscience." Such a principle of social and individual action, with its disregard of formal religion and established law, would have meant the destruction of the Puritan Commonwealth as it would mean the destruction of any other organized society; and Mrs. Hutchinson and two men were banished, while the firearms were taken away from their followers for fear that they might receive a private revelation to begin an armed rebellion. Whatever may be our modern repugnance to compulsion in religious matters, Roger Williams and Mrs. Hutchinson not only illustrate the operation of the authority of the Puritan Church over public life and morals; they make plain the fact that "the alternative to church law and order was fanaticism."

These events and banishments were before Increase Mather had appeared in the world; a quarter of a century before Cotton Mather was born. But they were vivid and effectual in the Puritan inheritance which the Mathers could not escape.

It was, therefore, in the very nature of their time and their religious duty as they conceived it, that the Mathers should be concerned with affairs of large moment in other fields than that of the Christian ministry and its theological enterprises. One of the notable episodes of American history but little reported by the historians is represented in the four years which Increase Mather spent in England, lobbying to recover the independence of the colony which had been lost when James II vacated the original charter granted by his grandfather James I. He fought, also, a long, difficult, and losing battle to preserve the original purity of purpose and government for Harvard College. Cotton Mather's life was largely passed in conflict for the pristine authority and severity of Puritanism as it had been maintained in the days of John Cotton and Richard Mather; and later he waged the warfare which most has given his name the not altogether merited shadow of obloquy, as he contended against whatever were the powers of darkness in the witchcraft period. But at all times these Mathers were preachers of unusual gifts and attainments of mind and character and with no common graces of the spiritual life.

Cotton Mather was the perfect embodiment of

the Puritan ideal in religion and the Christian ministry. He was an amazingly learned man. When he was but six months past eighteen years of age he took his Master's degree, his thesis being characteristically a defense of the proposition that the vowel points in Hebrew were of divine origin. At twenty-five he was in charge of one of the greatest churches of the colony, while his father was in England as agent for the colony opposing Charles II's demand that the Massachusetts charter be resigned into his hands. This was what Professor Barrett Wendell has said was the most important business ever yet confided to a native of New England. It must be kept in mind, however, that Professor Barrett wrote before Calvin Coolidge had succeeded to the Presidency and filled the White House with an atmosphere of New England that was as distinctive amid the political auras of Washington as it was ephemeral. At this same age of twenty-five Cotton Mather was considered the greatest scholar in America. He had read and was continually reading more books than any other American, and was beginning also to write books which, by the time of his death, had become so numerous as to make him even now an astonishment to less versatile minds. His spiritual eminence gave him a political leadership which no preacher since his time has had; and he exercised it, not always wisely, but always in the interest of the theocracy he was trying vainly to recover and the righteousness he was conscientiously attempting to enthrone.

He was religious to the point of what modern Protestantism would consider hopeless fanaticism, disciplining his mind and dealing with his body in such fashion that his candid diary reads at times like a report of the absurd. He had mystical experiences genuine enough not only to convince himself that he had communications from God, but fitting into the course of events so as to convince others of their reality.

He participated in the extreme forms of religious worship which seem particularly Puritan and grotesque to later generations, finding nothing to remark in the long sermons and prolonged public prayers of the time. On a day of deep concern for the colony, when James II was proclaimed king, and, as a result, Cotton Mather and two friends were giving themselves together to serious thought and exercises, he preached three sermons to them, each about an hour long. Ten days after he had been formally ordained, Judge Sewall—afterward one of the judges in the witchcraft trials—described what was known as a private fast in which the magistrates and their wives participated with the ministers. His diary records of the one service, two sermons, one by Cotton Mather, and four prayers of which one was also by Cotton Mather; and if four prayers seem to be rather few on such an occasion, the presumption will be somewhat relieved by the report which Judge Sewall gives of one of the prayers, that "Mr. Moody prayed about an hour and a half." That youth will be served, even in Puritan New England, is evident from Cotton Mather's report in his diary of a young people's thanksgiving, that the Lord helped him to preach unto them almost three hours, though he had little more than one hour's time to prepare for it. "And a good day it was!"

Puritan, mystic, scholar, politician that he was, he possessed also another quality which seems strangely out of keeping with the memory of him that has come down to us. In August, 1685, when he was between twenty-two and twenty-three years old, he records that he is praying "for the guidance and blessing of God in what concerns the change of my condition in the world, from single to married; whereto I have now many invitations." Nor was this popularity with the feminine Puritans confined to the days of his youth. He had, in the course of his years, three wives, and received one proposal of marriage from a beautiful young woman, when he was a widower nearly forty years old. As Stuart Sherman wrote, "He possessed that which the *Ladies' Home Journal* would describe as 'What Women Admire in Men.'"

His prayers for guidance recorded in the diary of his twenty-third year were evidently answered, for on the fourth of May on the year following he was married. He got up early that morning in order properly to meditate upon appropriate devotional themes, but nevertheless reached the scene of the marriage earlier than, as a bridegroom, he should have appeared. A good many modern preachers have done likewise on their wedding day though there are few records of early meditation, and fewer have occupied so homiletically the interval of waiting. He went out into the garden with his Bible and read the second chapter of the Gospel of Saint John, fetching, as he wrote in his inevitable diary, "one observation and one supplication out of every verse." It was fresh from such a mood that he was married, and in keeping with it that the change of his condition in the world, from single to married, did not interrupt his preaching for a single Sabbath.

A good man, religious, learned, ambitious, influential, attractive, human—all that was dangerous in the tendencies of his character and temperament, all that was sinister in the tyranny implicit in the theocratic ideal of which he was the protagonist, all that was ruthless in the austere theology which he held with unquestioned sincerity, came to the fore seven years later, in the witchcraft frenzy and the part which he played in the bitter tragedy it evoked. The details of that tragic era of New England history do not fall within the scope of this study; but it is well to recall, amid the incredible ignorance or unfairness of the more rabid critics of the Puritans, that when the worst has been disclosed, the madness at Salem was a very trifling episode in the long and melancholy history of witchcraft. The cruelty of the New-England Puritans, which is so often cited as if it were the supreme atrocity of misguided religion and narrow prejudice, is almost negligible in comparison with the ferocity, under like delusions, of other lands and other religionists across the centuries. The fact is that the New-England Puritans dealt more lightly with witchcraft than any other body of faith had done; and long after the New-England witch hunts were only a bad memory, witches and their torture were actual enterprises in Spain, Germany, and England. Only twenty people were put to death in New England while the delusion ran its brief course, and none was ever burned; though to read the recurring literature and oratory of accusation one would infer that from the Hudson to Casco Bay there had been a series of bonfires like Nero's famous human torches when burning Christians illuminated his garden party.

There can be no doubt that Cotton Mather was the most eminent and most influential of the men of his time in pressing the charges against the victims of the delusion and in demanding the severest penalties upon them. The state of public feeling and theological belief being what it was, it ought also to be said in fairness that not a few of the victims made any other course difficult, particularly for a public man who in all sincerity took his theology and his social responsibilities as seriously as Mather did. He has more than once been accused of hypocrisy, of sacrificing the victims of the delusion to the furtherance of his ambitions for power, of contriving the death of the innocent for the maintenance of his own leadership. Wiser historians have other views. He prosecuted the witches because he sincerely believed in the genuineness of witchcraft. The most ruthless of his public attitudes and actions had, as their concomitants, the most searching personal prayer, fastings, disciplines, and spiritual ecstasies in private. That he was superstitious to what to us is an incredible degree is evident. Judge Sewall, the most famous of the magistrates at the witchcraft trials, was no less so; and his was not a light, unbalanced, nor uninformed mind. What fails often to be considered in today's contemptuous criticism of the witch-hunting Puritans is witchcraft's implication in the Puritan theology and in what may be called the Puritan philosophy of history, the best brief exposition of which is probably Professor Barrett Wendell's chapter in his biography of Cotton Mather.

The Puritans believed quite simply and firmly that America had been under the uninterrupted rule of Satan until their arrival in 1620. If any proof were needed, they found it in the desperate physical and social miseries in which the Indians lived. The landing of the *Mayflower* passengers, guided, as they had been, by God in order to establish a theocracy the character and sanction of which they recognized in the Scriptures, was a direct attack upon this rule of Satan. Naturally, the Evil One opposed it by all the means at his command. The bitter experiences of the first settlers—famine, pestilence, inclement weather, the recreancy of heretics and the malice of Indians—were all and alike the work of Satanic animosity. During the storms of the time church steeples were again and again struck by lightning, and Mather records the incidents in his journal as the devil's own work.

Back of this simple but powerful belief in the malignant activity of a personal devil there were, on the one hand, scriptural authority and examples of witchcraft and, on the other, the long, sinister history of black arts, demoniac possession and the most extreme punishments of witches, in Europe. The books, old and new, were not without almost innumerable instances of men and women whom Satan, in one form or another, had bought or forced into his service.

> Whoever yielded to him was rewarded by the possession of supernatural power, which was secretly exerted for all manner of malicious purposes; these were the witches: whoever withstood him was tortured in mind and body almost beyond the power of men to bear; these were the bewitched.[2]

The most terrible aspect of the diabolism was the ever-present possibility that it might establish itself, as, indeed, it did manifest itself, within the Church. Laymen and ministers alike might be secretly possessed, so that their appalling state might be that of desperate apostasy from their Lord.

Professor Wendell's distinctive explanation of the phenomena is so discerning and suggestive that it deserves to be given in full, though one must remember that the witchcraft frenzy appeared long before modern psychology, which goes back

[2] Barrett Wendell: *Cotton Mather,* p. 92.

only three generations. The Puritans, accordingly, could not have made any such explanation, but on the other hand they would not have felt any need for any such an explanation; they rested their case on the Old Testament. Professor Wendell writes:

> If, as modern science tends to show, human beings are the result of a process of evolution from lower forms of life, there must have been in our ancestral history a period when the intelligence of our progenitors was as different from the modern human mind—the only form of intelligence familiar to our experience or preserved in the records of our race—as were their remote aquatic bodies from the human form today. Today we can perceive with any approach to distinctness only what reveals itself to us through the medium of our five senses; but we have only to look at the intricate wheelings of a flock of birds, at the flight of a carrier pigeon, at the course of a dog who runs straight home over a hundred miles of strange country, to see more than a probability that animals not remote from us physically have perceptions to which we are strangers. It seems wholly conceivable, then, that in the remote psychologic past of our race there may have been in our ancestors certain powers of perception which doubtless centuries of disuse have made so rudimentary that in our normal condition we are not conscious of them. But if such there were, it would not be strange that, in abnormal states, the rudimentary vestiges of these disused powers of perception might sometimes be revived. If this were the case, we might naturally expect two phenomena to accompany such a revival: in the first place, as such powers of perception, from my very hypothesis, belong normally to a period in the development of our race when human society and what we call moral law

have not yet appeared, we should expect them to be intimately connected with a state of emotion that ignores what we call the moral sense, and so accompanied by various forms of misconduct; in the second place, as our chief modern means of communication—articulate language—belongs to a period when human intelligence has assumed its present form, we should expect to find it inadequate for the expression of facts which it never professed to cover, and so we should expect such phenomena as we are considering to be accompanied by an erratic, impotent inaccuracy of statement, which anyone who believes in a personal devil would not hesitate to ascribe to the direct intervention of Satan.

Now, what disposes me . . . to think that my guess may have something in it is that mental and moral degeneracy—credulity and fraud—seem almost invariably so to entangle themselves with occult phenomena that many cool-headed people are disposed to assert the whole thing a lie. To me, as I have shown, it does not seem so simple. I am much disposed to think that necromancers, witches, mediums—what not—actually do perceive in the infinite realities about us things that are imperceptible to normal human beings; but that they perceive them only at a sacrifice of their higher faculties—mental and moral—not inaptly symbolized in the old tales of those who sell their souls.

If this be true, witchcraft is not a delusion: it is a thing more subtly dangerous still. Such an epidemic of it as came to New England in 1692 is as diabolical a fact as human beings can know: unchecked, it can really work mischief unspeakable. I have said enough, I think, to show why I heartily sympathize with those who in 1692 did their utmost to suppress it; to show too why the fatally tragic phase of the witch trials seems to me, not the fact that there was no crime to condemn, but the fact that the evidence on which certain wretched people were executed proves, on scrutiny, utterly insufficient. It was little better than today would be the ravings of a clairvoyant against one accused of theft. And yet, if there be anything in my guess, this too is just what we might expect. Not knowing what they did, the judges would strain every nerve—just as in their rapt ecstasies the Mathers strained every nerve, along with their Puritan fellows, and the saints of every faith—to awaken from the lethargy of countless ages those rudimentary powers which can be awakened only at the expense of what we think the higher ones that have supplanted them. The motive may make a difference: he who strives to serve God may end as he began, a better man than he who consents to serve the devil. But, for all that, bewitched and judges alike, the startled ministers to whom the judges turned for counsel, and perhaps not a few of the witches too, who may well have believed in themselves, vie with one another in a devil's race, harking back to mental and moral depths from which humanity has taken countless centuries to rise.[3]

This is neither the theory nor the language which Cotton Mather could have used, a century and three quarters before Darwin; and it may be that even so distinguished a thinker as Professor Wendell has not satisfactorily explained the phenomena; though I confess that his hypothesis seems to me to be by no means without plausibility. But Cotton Mather, with his prescientific theology and whatever may have been the intolerance, hypocrisy, and self-seeking which later historians have

---

[3] Barrett Wendell: *Cotton Mather,* pp. 95ff.

charged against him, believed sincerely that the phenomena he had before his eyes constituted "as diabolical a fact as human beings can know," and that if it were unchecked it would work mischief unspeakable.

For he was committed by all his intelligence, inheritance, education and emotion, to the theology with which witchcraft's awful and tragic mystery, as well as the political theocracy for which he strove, was involved. The general character of that theology is casually familiar; but neither the Mathers, nor the conflict and failure of the Puritanism which they incarnated, nor the significance of progressive religious thought since their day, can be appreciated unless something of the inclusiveness and definiteness of their stern creed be brought to mind. The initial article of faith to which Puritanism and, indeed, all Christianity subscribed until the vast upheaval of *The Origin of Species* and *The Descent of Man,* was that God by arbitrary fiat had created Adam and Eve who disobeyed His specific commandment and so "fell," bringing, not simply upon themselves but upon their descendants, eternal punishment.

As a result, all men thereafter, while inexorably responsible for doing the will of God, were forever incapable of doing it. God, however, sent His Son in the person of Jesus who by giving Himself to death on the cross became a ransom, not—notwithstanding the explicit utterance of the New Testament—for all, but for only that portion of humanity which God, for His own inscrutable glory, should choose unto salvation. No human mind could identify the elect. There were no irrefutable evidences upon which human judgment could rely. Anyone might be of the fortunate number and, conversely, anyone might be of those whom the divine election passed by. But whoever was of the elect would be able to do the will of God which was to be found revealed in the Bible. It was the duty, therefore, of everyone who could do the will of God as revealed therein to persevere in the performance of it, and so to build up whatever assurances were possible, cultivating the holiest aspirations, maintaining the severest self-disciplines, venturing upon the most demanding and rewarding experiences that seemed to be of grace. There could be no invincible assurance, of course, for only God knew the elect. But those who gave themselves to lives of such exacting devotion might indulge the hope that the mercy of God would ultimately include them in its benefits.

Nothing less than a volume could adequately present that original American Puritanism for which the Mathers stood, to maintain which they fought out their lives. An austere religion, narrow, dim in hope and almost fierce in its outlook upon life and eternity; socially intolerant and politically an attempt to re-establish a way of life that ended with the Roman conquest of Palestine, the universe was against it. The very Protestantism of the Puritans fought like Sisera's stars against them. For the genius of Protestantism is progress. When it halts the mind or seeks to establish a fixed and finished faith and order, it ceases to be Protestantism and becomes its own Nemesis. The Puritanism of John Cotton and the Mathers had to fail; and the story of that failure, through generations of sincere Christians, through a long line of prophetic preachers, is the story of our present-day inheritance of devout free thought.

References

Adams, James T., *The Founding of New England.*

Boas, Ralph P., *Cotton Mather, Keeper of the Puritan Conscience.*

Byington, E. H., *The Puritan in England and in New England.*

Chamberlain, N. H., *Samuel Sewall and the World He Lived In.*

Drake, S. G., *Witchcraft Delusion in New England.*

Eggleston, Edward, *The Beginners of a Nation.*

Ellis, G. E., *The Puritan Age and Rule in the Colony of Massachusetts Bay.*

Hanscom, Elizabeth D., ed., *The Heart of the Puritan.*

Howe, D. W., *The Puritan Republic.*

Marvin, Abijan P., *The Life and Times of Cotton Mather.*

Morison, Samuel E., *Builders of the Bay Colony.*

Murdock, K. B., *Increase Mather.*

Parrington, Vernon L., *Main Currents in American Thought.*

Schneider, Herbert W., *The Puritan Mind.*

Wendell, Barrett, *Cotton Mather, the Puritan Priest.*

II

JONATHAN EDWARDS, HIS GOD

II

JONATHAN EDWARDS, HIS GOD

THERE are phrases like prisms, transforming what has seemed to be a monotonous tradition into vivid and revealing colors. Such a phrase is "the Great Awakening," which illumines as it suggests one of the more significant events of American religious history. The Great Awakening, however, was an episode rather than an event, continuing in New England, from 1734 to 1736, and then, after an interval of subsidence, recovering new vigor for another period of two years. It was probably the most dramatic and violent revival of religion which ever swept across any considerable portion of the American continent. Within a space of those few years forty thousand people were added to the churches of New England and the other colonies; and when one realizes how sparsely populated were the colonies two hundred years ago, those figures tell a remarkable tale. What perhaps is as extraordinary as the sweep and passion of the movement is that it was a revival of conversion under the preaching of a theology which did not recognize experience as a witness of assurance and declared fundamentally that men had no initiative in their salvation, but that it was wholly of an arbitrary God who chose some for eternal bliss while the vaster majority of the race he determined for eternal doom, all for the maintenance of his own sublimer glory. It was a revival comparable in mood and power to the tumultuous revivals of later years, though on a much wider scale; as when, for instance, the preaching of Moody declared the love of God and invited men and women to his universal compassion. The stormy enthusiasm of the Great Awakening, continuing for two strenuous and highly emotional years, was filled with excesses, physical demonstrations, episodes of madness, but always with tremendous power, and it ended almost as suddenly as it had begun, apparently from sheer exhaustion. But it put its stamp upon American life and disclosed and revivified a spirit which has had something to do with the more heroic quality in earlier American character; and it began with the preaching of one man, whose life united vicissitudes of fame and neglect, at the time some thirty-one years old, in the highly esteemed and more than ordinarily cultured Congregational pulpit of Northampton, Massachusetts.

Northampton, Massachusetts, is now famous for more than one of its possessions. It is the seat of Smith College, though it has lost the luster borrowed for a time from that loquacious professor whose ideas on a good many things were among the curious and monitory exhibitions of what a vivid imagination will sometimes do when substituted for sound knowledge. But the proudest landmark to which a thoughtful traveler used to be directed was the little, simple old house—now destroyed to make place for a gasoline station—in which, for twenty-three years, lived Jonathan Edwards, whose preaching began the Great Revival and who remains, after the one hundred and seventy-seven years which have passed above his grave, the most powerful intellect which America has yet produced. He was born at East Windsor, Connecticut, in October, 1703, five months after John Wesley was born at Epworth, England; and it is, perhaps, not wholly a coincidence in the providences of God that the Great Revival of the Wesleys, in England, began just three years after the Great Awakening initiated by Edwards in America had spent itself.

There are few, if any, competent students who will deny that Jonathan Edwards was the most powerful intellect America has yet produced; and while it is not necessary, it is well to see the human stuff of which he was a part. It began when a young woman named Elizabeth Tuttle, both of whose parents were English and whose father was said to be more than nobly born, married a Hartford attorney named Richard Edwards. She was widely known not only for her beauty but for her unusual intelligence. This Richard Edwards at the time, which was 1667, was a man of great repute in New England. Twenty-four years later he secured a divorce from his brilliant and beautiful wife on supported charges of flagrant immorality—a seventeenth-century indication that intellect and character are not inevitable companions. After his divorce Richard Edwards married again, having by this second marriage five sons and one daughter, none of whom ever rose above mediocrity and none of whose descendants ever achieved any reputation.

But his first wife, this Elizabeth Tuttle, was the mother of a son named Timothy Edwards, who graduated from Harvard College, gaining both the Bachelor's and Master's degrees at the one Commencement, in the same year that his parents were divorced. In due time this Timothy Edwards was installed as the minister of the church at East Windsor, Connecticut, where he remained for forty-nine years, becoming the father of eleven children, one of whom was Jonathan Edwards. It is now an old story, but one not yet without significance, that in 1900, thirteen hundred and ninety-four of Jonathan Edwards's descendants had been identified and their careers reported. Two hundred and ninety-five were college graduates; thirteen were presidents of colleges, with many others principals of similar institutions; more than one hundred of them were clergymen, missionaries, and theological professors; seventy-five were officers in the army and navy; sixty were prominent authors and writers, having produced one hundred and thirty-five important books and edited eighteen publications; sixty were physicians; more than one hundred were lawyers, one a very eminent professor of law; thirty were judges; eighty held public office, one being a Vice-President of the United States. Three were United States senators, others being members of Congress, mayors of cities, and ministers to foreign governments, and others prominent in business and banking; while none has been reported as having been convicted of crime.

This is the family which sprang from Jonathan Edwards; from whose origins he arose; and it is no surprise, then, to read that a paper which he wrote, when he was only twelve years old, on a study of American spiders, was received by the Royal Society of Great Britain and was the beginning of nature study in America; that his studies on the mind, written when he was sixteen, were sound enough to be repeated in one of his books written when he was fifty; that he entered Yale College at the age of thirteen and graduated at seventeen, though of course it was not the thorough and advanced curriculum which would be required now. This is the man, tall, spare, solemn, who stamped American religious and philosophical thinking for a hundred and fifty years with the likeness of his own mind. Of him, George A. Gordon, the vindication of whose theology one hundred and fifty years later marked the final overthrow of Edwards's doctrinal system, said:

> He is perhaps the only American intellect that deserves a place in the ranks of the world's great thinkers. We can be sure that his name is among the kings; we can not be sure that another name in our history is there.[1]

I

None of us, probably, is greatly interested in the details of Edwards's life; it is the character of the

[1] Hoyt, *Pulpit and American Life,* p. 19.

man and the quality of his religious belief which left their impress so long upon the generations after him, which concern us. In keeping with that, it is natural to discover that he was as extraordinary in his religious as in his intellectual life. Before he was nineteen he wrote and kept a series of seventy resolutions governing his personal conduct and experience, which have been widely quoted. One of them, for instance, was, "Resolved, never to do any manner of thing, whether in soul or body, less, or more, but that tends to the glory of God, nor be nor suffer it, if I can possibly avoid it." Another was, "Resolved, to live with all my might, while I do live." Still another was, "Resolved, never to do anything which I should be afraid to do if it were the last hour of my life." So his resolutions ran which, to the best of his ability, he kept throughout his life. There were two others of them at least in which men and women today might find, perhaps, the secret of their own unsatisfactory religious life: "Resolved, to examine carefully and constantly what one thing in me is, which causes me in the least to doubt the love of God; and to direct all my forces against it;" and, "Resolved, to cast away such things as I find do abate my assurance."

A hundred and twenty-five years before William James was born—William James and his argument for the will to believe, who coined the phrase and argued the philosophy—nineteen-year-old Jonathan Edwards had hit upon the necessity of the will to believe and was disciplining his mind to choose the highest ends of life and faith. And the religious lapses of multitudes of men and women today, the disintegration of their faith, can be traced to their failure to think intelligently through their religious experiences, to face honestly the causes of their doubts, to direct their energies of mind and life and spirit against the recognized enemies of belief and satisfaction. What Socrates said twenty-five hundred years ago is still true, that there is danger in the unexamined life.

But here, in this young man's determination to exclude everything that caused him to doubt the love of God, is the supreme paradox and contradiction of the man through all his years. In his personal religious experience, in his private writings and testimonies, he enjoyed to a remarkable degree what he was sure was the love of God; but he preached the most terrible doctrine of God that ever left the lips or lingered in the minds of men. No creed was ever so bad but saintly men have held it; none was ever so good but that it sheltered base souls. In his *Journal* Jonathan Edwards tells the difficulty with which he reached his own belief. John Wesley came to his transforming religious experience, as he himself wrote, while he heard Luther's preface to the Epistle to the Romans being read aloud, in a little gathering in Aldersgate Street, London, at a quarter before nine on the evening of May 24, 1738. Likewise Jonathan Edwards, telling how as a young man he rebelled again and again against the thought of the absolute sovereignty of God, wrote in his *Journal* that when he was about twenty years old, as he was reading the words in the New Testament: "Now unto the King eternal, immortal, invisible, the only wise God, be honor and glory forever and ever, Amen," there came into his soul a sense of the glory of the Divine Being; and from then on he was sure of the unchanging, unconditioned, and awful sovereignty of God. What was God's absolute will was the one end of his life, as it was for all of Calvinism; and it became part of that New-England idea of religion and of holiness as Edwards influenced it, and Samuel Hopkins phrased it, to be willing to be damned if God should wish it. Candidates for church membership, and candidates for the ministry were publicly asked if they were so willing; and theoretically, at least, no one could know but that he was elected to what our most brilliant essayist on Jonathan Edwards calls his "pleasant, bright, and sweet doctrine of damnation."

It is not within the scope of this chapter to discuss in any detail his personal life and diverse fortunes, but it must be said that in his theology and in his study his wife was almost as remarkable as he; and to read the story of their life together is to discover underneath the terrible austerity of the New-England Calvinist a romance as true as it was sedate. His wife came even more directly than he did to that awful willingness to be damned for the glory of God, but her character was such that those who knew her said that she had found a shorter way to heaven than her husband. She made it her lifework to protect him from all demands that would distract his studies, so far as she could accomplish it. He spent thirteen hours a day in his study; his only recreation being horseback riding or walking in the woods; and then it was his custom to carry with him pen and ink and paper. When he thought of something worth considering again, he would stop and write it out; and it is said that he would return with his bits of paper pinned to various parts of his clothes, a sight for scholars and an example to his flock. So his time passed in Northampton, first as assistant to his mother's father in the pastorate of the church, then as minister himself. So he came to 1734, one hundred and fourteen years after the landing of the *Mayflower*.

At this time the old, sterner Calvinism of the past was already changing. Since the harsh predestination of the Puritans ascribing salvation to the sheer, inaccessible will of God, with nothing for men to do but accept their fate, men had begun to ask what they could do to put themselves in such a position that God might save them. Accordingly, they had given themselves to prayer and Bible reading and church attendance, not as works of salvation but as means by which God might be influenced toward them. As time passed they had drifted into the belief, a very human and natural procedure, that these duties really constituted religion itself; and some had begun to go yet further, and to speak and to conduct themselves as if the Christian life were but the practice of morality and as if what is needed is not the transformation of character but the education of the mind. It was in such moods as these that his congregation with no great concern heard Jonathan Edwards preaching against their complacency for some seven years after his coming to their pulpit. Then, in 1734, two sudden deaths in the little town disturbed the conventional religionists with the thought that their mild religion was a sign that God had withdrawn Himself; and Jonathan Edwards began that series of sermons which shook a continent and echoed in the British Isles, in which he declared with terrible and even ferocious extremities of language the awful sovereignty of God, the complete enmity and estrangement of mankind from Him, the desperate and unrelieved wickedness of all men, and God's right and purpose to do as He pleased with His creatures; and while sometimes he preached the blessedness of being right with God, generally it was the utter worthlessness of all human good and the terrors of the world to come that he proclaimed.

He had none of the arts of the orator. He wrote his sermons and read them, his gestures being hardly more than those which he used in turning the leaves of his manuscript as he read. His voice was even and quiet and well modulated, but what he said inaugurated an epidemic of suicides, one of his own members being among them, and many others confessing to be tempted. There were larger results of course. Within six months three hundred people in the little town had been converted and the whole tone of life was changed, for at the time there were not more than two hundred families in Northampton. A biographer writing almost one hundred years ago said, with what sounds like a curious echo of more modern social criticism, that the habits of the young people which for years had given so much uneasiness to the best people of the Church, were laid aside. On beyond Northampton, in many other towns, the movement spread. Men in England were interested and Edwards was in correspondence with others throughout all the colonies and the British Isles as well. His preaching had reached and was yet to reach throughout the English-speaking world.

II

What, then, was that preaching like which, coming in quiet tones from an almost motionless, ascetic figure in a little, old-fashioned New England meetinghouse, left its stamp upon tens of thousands of lives and gave new life for at least a century to a theology that had been already dying? Nothing could be sublimer, someone wrote, "than Edwards's conception of God at his best; nothing could be more incredible than the treatment to which he subjects the race under God." Preaching on the text from Isaiah, "I will tread them in mine anger, and trample them in my fury, and their blood shall be sprinkled upon my garments, and I will stain all my raiment," he said: "If you cry to God to pity you, he will be so far from pitying you in your doleful case, or showing you the least regard or favor, that instead of that he will only tread you under foot: and though he will know that you cannot bear the weight of Omnipotence treading upon you, yet he will not regard that, but he will crush you under his feet without mercy; he will crush out your blood and make it fly, and it shall be sprinkled on his garments, so as to stain all his raiment. He will not only hate you, but he will have you in the utmost contempt; no place shall be thought fit for you but under his feet, to be trodden down as the mire in the streets."

In another often quoted sermon he described the damned glowing in unending agony as God holds them in eternal flame as a cruel boy might hold a spider over a blaze; and then he suggests that the felicity of the saints in heaven is heightened because they can look down and see the wicked in torment. He declared that little children, unless they are consciously in Christ, are as loathsome to God as vipers. Too much importance need not be given to this kindly doctrine, for he had eleven of them in his home and apparently never thought of them as vipers. To give one more example, perhaps his most famous, from his sermon on "Sinners in the Hands of an Angry God": "But to help your conception, imagine yourself to be cast into a fiery oven, all of a glowing heat, or into the midst of a glowing brick-kiln, or of a great furnace, where your pain would be much greater than that occasioned by accidentally touching a coal of fire, as the heat is greater. Imagine also that your body were to lie there for a quarter of an hour, full of fire, as full within and without as a bright coal of fire, all the while full of quick sense; what horror would you feel at the entrance of such a furnace! And how long would that quarter of an hour seem to you! If it were to be measured by a glass, how long would the glass seem to be running! And after you had endured it for one minute, think how overbearing it would be to think that you had it to endure the other fourteen." And from then he goes on lengthening the minutes to hours and years and millions of years. A minister who heard him preach this sermon tugged at Edwards's coat and cried out in terror, "Oh, Mr. Edwards, is not God a God of mercy?" No wonder that Oliver Wendell Holmes said that the dogma for which Jonathan Edwards fought all his life was one no decent man could hold without going crazy. For people did go crazy because of it.

But it is not enough, and certainly it is no mark of wisdom, to inquire, How could a man preach this dogma in this terrible fashion? He preached it because he believed it; and for three hundred and fifty years hundreds of thousands of men and women believed it, in varying degrees of intensity, satisfaction, and terror. It was the faith and doctrine of John Calvin. It was the passionate belief of John Knox. It was the creed of John Bunyan and Oliver Cromwell. It was the faith of the

Pilgrim Fathers and the great Independent body in England and Scotland from whom they came. For it Covenanters gave their lives before the bullets of Charles Second's soldiers, on the scaffolds of his venal courts, in the torture chambers of his cruel officers. And a faith which has sustained men and women through generation after generation of perplexed and heroic living and more heroic dying cannot be dismissed with the quick remark that no decent man could hold it without going crazy. It produced great lives, it upheld men and women through terrible sufferings, it strengthened them to walk through martyrdoms with music on their lips. It gave them courage to endure the hardships of this life, losses, betrayals, disasters, unrelieved poverty and biting, breaking, ill-rewarded labor, without complaint. In this faith, for all the contradiction of it, men and women grew to be tender and kind and sacrificial. It inspired them to make their homes serene, secure, and godly and to keep them rich in humility and affection. It strengthened them to reform their governments and rebuke their kings. It helped them abandon wealth and accept destitution rather than dishonor conscience. It carried them over strange seas and labored with them at the founding of the American Commonwealth. And for serious minds, genuinely concerned for present-day morality rather than in retrospect upon the frenzies of the Great Awakening, it is worth while to see what Jonathan Edwards's God really meant to human life.

III

First, at least in our thought of it, this terrible doctrine of an unpitying God and what logically and scripturally is an inexorable hell, supported a very sound though exaggerated sense of the reality of sin. It is altogether impossible for us to go back to the overwhelming emphasis on sin which the theology and religious experience of former generations maintained; because wiser insights into human life, surer understanding of the Scriptures and their place in the development of religion, the contribution which science has made to our knowledge of the world of which we are part and of ourselves, have changed the very bases of our ideas. We have and must keep much higher views of human nature than this theology of Edwards has cherished. But it is possible—in fact, it seems quite certain—that in our generation's revolt from the sternness of the past, in its uncritical acceptance of the most comfortable and liberating inferences of modern science, it and an untheological religion have gone altogether too far to the opposite extreme. Social Democracy has made our theology too timid.

There are certain ugly things of conduct, imagination, and experience which we recognize as bad. Some novelists, some materialistic minds in bondage to the animal part of us, might deny such a premise, but for the vast majority of us the reality of evil in speech or deed or imagination, does exist. We recognize also that there are actions and words uttered which, in themselves, are wrong. They can be identified, named, remembered. A lie told; a blow struck; the theft of a possession—these things are definite and definitely wrong. And that is about as far as a modern man goes in the way of recognizing the fact of sin. As a result, when he feels sorry for having committed anything of the kind; when he makes up for it as best he can by a new kindness, by repaying the loss, or resolving that he will never do it again; the modern man has done about all that he thinks it necessary to do. And he is tremendously mistaken. Because while he quits one kind of wrong, he finds himself doing another. Back of the occasional deed is the constant trend; and the process is one of endless failure. We no longer hold to the older doctrine of original sin; the Puritan's idea of it is as dead as the dodo. But in that carefully wrought and almost hopeless dogma the Puritan, the New England Calvinist, had an insight much deeper than may appear to casual modern dissidents. He was not terribly burdened because of the comparatively few wrong things which he did. They were bad and he repented of them; but the hopeless heart of the matter was that they were just the surface evidences of a malady that affected his whole existence. What troubled him was not that he *did* wrong but that he *was* wrong, and completely wrong. As a clever student of religion has put it: "His moral problem was not to keep his petty cash account with God balanced week by week. What haunted his soul was the knowledge that there was a mortgage on the whole business."[2] Like Paul, he was sold under sin; and there was no hope for him except in the sheer, unreasonable, undiscoverable, inaccessible election of God; while for those not elected—and who could tell?—the awfulness of the reprobate other world was the natural expectation.

We cannot and surely ought not to go back to that terrible theology; but we shall have little moral safety and less hope for a world and society of moral beauty until we recover the conviction that evil is not a matter of act only but fundamentally is a disease of character; that the great test of life is not alone what we do but what we are; and that the fatality of evil deeds is that they are the fruitage of evil will. We deny the old affirmations of original sin. Certainly we do not believe that

"In Adam's fall
We sinned all."

But the Puritan's theology represented a reasoned and commanding answer to personal experience of sin. He accounted for its unmistakable reality and offered a sure though appalling treatment of it. Whatever we are, we are not what we ought to be; and only in the hope of God's doing something for us that we cannot do for ourselves can we ever come back to satisfaction and moral strength. That is one direction in which Jonathan Edwards's God still points the way.

---

[2] Sperry: *Disciplines of Liberty*, p. 66.

Then again, this stern, omnipotent sovereignty of God, in the very least as well as the very largest enterprises and aspects of life, was an answer to the inescapable demand of human need for responsible authority. Much has been said in recent years of the New Humanism, which in many quarters has been regarded as the most dangerous contemporary attack upon religion. The essence of humanistic theology is that God is but the name we have given to the ideals which mankind itself has won in its struggle through time. It is a complimentary and not unappealing theory. But it fails precisely at the point where the average man wants success, namely, at the point of an assurance that he is not only progressing but that he is progressing toward a right end. Humanism tells us simply that we are on the way, but nobody knows whither or that we shall ever get anywhere. Dismissing immortality as an idle superstition, the Humanists say in effect, though not in the precise language, "We are not going anywhere; we are just going around."

Jonathan Edwards's God, the God of centuries of our forebears in the heroic times in Scotland, England, America, and on the Continent, was undoubtedly a very harsh and awful God. He chose men to honor and dishonor, elected a few to salvation and many to hell, and tramped terribly over the helpless creatures of His own creation. But one thing was certain: He knew where He was going and the world was not adrift. The destiny of men for the most part was awful but it was unmistakable. Men might be unhappy, but they were sure; and, of course, there were the multitudes like Edwards who personally lived in the sense of blessédness with God. The latest biographer of Carlyle tells a characteristic incident of old David Hope, a Scotch farmer:

> In Hope's locality the harvests were late and often hard to save, when all-day rains continued week after week, and gain or loss for the farmer depended on intervals of a day or two, "during which the moments are golden." On one such morning old David was in haste to be afield. The breakfast porridge was speedily dispatched. Then as the Bible was opened for family worship, somebody came in crying "Such a raging wind has risen: will drive the stooks into the sea if let alone!"
>
> "Wind?" answered David. "Wind canna get ae straw that has been appointed mine. Sit down, and let us worship God."[3]

For the Calvinist, the Edwardist, a sublime authority spoke through every item and aspect of nature, time, and experience. And without dwelling on that point it remains true that one of the primary needs of life is the sense of authority for the world, the conviction and assurance that with all this welter of evil in it, anarchies of thought and discords of society and nations, the world is not mindless and unguided. When Garfield was shot, did not Blaine telegraph, "God reigns, and the government at Washington still lives"? It is

[3] Wilson: *Carlyle,* Vol. I, p. 34.

that conviction which New-England theology emphasized, that God reigns, which this turbulent and changing time of ours most needs.

With these two great contributions to human life and thought—the reality of sin and the reality and sovereignty of God—in spite of the awfulness of the consequences which it gathered to them, this New-England theology enabled men to live heroically, and because no creed is so bad but saintly men and women have held it, New-England men and women were kindly, reverent, and good, as well as firm.

But that theology and Jonathan Edwards, its chief spokesman for a century and a half, because of these perhaps natural but nevertheless unfortunate misconceptions of Scripture, terribly misrepresented God, and so did the world immense disservice. God is sovereign, but not over us as a tyrant but through us and with us as a Friend. He is not a Monarch as Edwards pictured Him; He is the Father of our Lord Jesus Christ. He is not like Isaiah's warrior trampling enemies in his fury; He is like Jesus; and the supreme word to describe Him is not "wrath" but "love." Turn back to one of Ian Maclaren's stories of the old Scottish Glen of Drumtochty, and those hard-bitten Calvinists whose character is the granite on which four hundred years of Scotland has been built. He tells, doubtless out of his own personal tradition, that "there had been a revival man there and he was preaching on hell. As it grew dark a candle was lighted and showed his face as that of a hard-visaged man. He looked down at the little boys on the front bench of the bare little meetinghouse, and asked them if they knew what hell was. By that time they were so terrified they could not speak but one of them whispered 'No!' "

Then he rolled up a piece of paper and held it in the flame, and they saw it burn and glow and shrivel up, and fall in black dust.

"Think," he said, and he leaned over the desk and spoke in a gruesome whisper which made the cold chills run down the little boys' backs, "that yon paper was your finger, one finger only of your hand, and it burned like that forever and ever, and think of your hand and your whole body all on fire, never to go out." The boys shuddered so you might have heard the bench creak. "That is hell," the preacher went on, "and that is where ony laddie will go who does not repent and believe."

Then he blew out the candle, and as the congregation went out the frightened boys crept to the door trembling and unable to say a word. That night one of the boys couldn't sleep, for he kept thinking of the fire he might be in by morning. He looked out of the window and saw the oat stacks standing in rows and they made him think of the Judgment, and the little boy cried for his mother. When she came in, he told her about it, and she had heard the sermon, and Calvinist though she was, almost hated the preacher, and the little boy held his arms around her neck and kept asking, "Is yon God? Is yon God?" And his mother told him he was safe with her, and that while God might punish him to make him better, God would never torture anybody, that was the devil's work; and then she asked him, "Am I a guid mother tae ye?" He couldn't say anything, he could just hold his mother hard, but she understood and said, "Be sure God maun be a hantle kinder." So the truth came home even to a little Scotch boy in a Calvinist family and he fell asleep in the love of God.

God as "a hantle kinder" is no Edwardian phrase. The words are not at home in the vocabulary of eighteenth-century Calvinism in New England. That Calvinism was a religion of iron and granite, and no one can overestimate its contribution to life in days when almost incredible hardships challenged faith in the Eternal with the hostility of time. But even while Edwards and his New-England colleagues proclaimed the terrors of the Almighty, other voices were rising with the most characteristic New-Testament declaration of the God and Father of our Lord Jesus Christ.

It is the purpose of succeeding chapters to portray some of the men of New England and elsewhere and their distinctive services, by whom we have been led into that more liberal faith and confidence.

References

Allen, A. V. G., *Jonathan Edwards.*

Gewehr, W. M., *The Great Awakening in Virginia, 1740-1790.*

Maxson, C. H., *The Great Awakening in the Middle Colonies.*
McGiffert, A. C., *Jonathan Edwards.*
Parkes, Harry B., *Jonathan Edwards, the Fiery Puritan.*
Tracy, Joseph, *The Great Awakening.*
Wright, A., *Life and Character of Jonathan Edwards.*

III

GEORGE WHITEFIELD AND HIS MASTER'S VOICE

III

GEORGE WHITEFIELD AND HIS MASTER'S VOICE

George Whitefield belongs in any study of New-England theology, however casual, although in life he was neither a New Englander nor a theologian. He was an Englishman by race and rearing; by birth, residence, and affection; and the total time he spent in America during his life was but little indeed compared to the years he passed in the land of his birth. His most striking American monument is not in New England today; it is on the campus of the University of Pennsylvania, in Philadelphia. You may see it there, in front of the dormitory triangle, erected by University alumni who were Methodists. His chief American responsibility was an orphanage in Georgia, of which some reminders still remain and which, while never home in any rich and familiar sense, was, perhaps, the nearest to being his home of any place on earth after he left the English inn where first history finds him. He *is* a New Englander, however, by reason of his unintentional contribution to the forces which disintegrated the New-England theology, and a New Englander in death, as Newburyport, Massachusetts, will testify.

There, in that old seaport city, is the South Presbyterian Church, in itself a strangely haunted house for one sensitive to the spirit of the past. In its aisles was enrolled the first company of rebel patriots for the Revolutionary War. Beneath and behind its high pulpit is a beautiful old seat taken from a pirate ship, of the old buccaneering days. Unfortunately, it is not the only church in which a thoughtful Christian can find mementos of buccaneers. Just behind the church is the house in which William Lloyd Garrison was born; and, more appropriate for the purposes of this chapter, in its quiet old back rooms are chairs, a table, a traveling desk, and other articles which once belonged to George Whitefield, together with mementos, from America and England, of his blazing career; and the dignified old Negro sexton will reverently show the visitor the big Bible which Whitefield carried around with him, as large as a pulpit Bible, scarred with hard usage and worn thin and ragged at his favorite text. But that is by no means all the old church holds. It has what, on the other side of the sea, might, by a great stretch of the imagination, be called a crypt. The sexton will take one down into the cellar, in a dark passage and into a darker room which he lights with a feeble electric light. Then he opens a small door in a brick or stone side of a built-up sort of bin, the door reached by a few wooden steps, and puts a flashlight into one's hand. The hardy-minded visitor stoops inside and sees a very rude brick sarcophagus with a glass top; and if his courage does not fail in the eerie atmosphere and he looks inside the box, he will see the fragments of three skeletons, two being the remains of former ministers of the church, the third and largest—just a few bones and a blackened skull—being that of George Whitefield himself, who died in a home still standing hard by the church, on the morning of September thirtieth, six years before the Declaration of Independence.

One of the familiar legends tells that on the afternoon of the Crucifixion sailors on the Aegean Sea found themselves suddenly in the midst of darkness while a great voice mourned from the purple shores, "Pan is dead!"

> "Calm of old, the bark went onward,
> When a cry more loud than wind,
> Rose up, deepened, and swept sunward,
> From the pilèd Dark behind;
> And the sun shrank, and grew pale
> Breathed against by the great wail—
> 'Pan, Pan is dead.' "

It is history that the boy Alfred Tennyson, when the news came back to England that Byron had succumbed to fever in far-off Greece, carved upon a tree in the old garden at Somersby, the words, "Byron is Dead," and felt as if the day had closed. It is history also, and by no means a legend, that on the Sunday after Whitefield fell asleep and a messenger galloped into Portsmouth crying, "Whitefield is dead!" he was heard by a young man named Benjamin Randall who had listened to Whitefield preaching in Portsmouth two days before he died, and had turned away. Randall himself told later that it was not only the messenger be heard, but, said he, "a voice sounded through my soul more loud and startling than ever thunder pealed upon my ears, 'Whitefield is dead.' " His own thought was: "Whitefield is now in heaven, but I am on the road to hell. O that I could hear his voice again!" The dead Whitefield still spoke to him; and here follows one of the paradoxes of theological continuity. The man converted through his memory of the preaching of a Calvinistic Methodist became the founder of the Free-Will Baptists.

The story of George Whitefield is a record of Providence, a romance of a single gift dedicated to God until the greatest orator of his generation was but his Master's voice. He was born in the old English city of Gloucester, no mean city in literature or history or religion. Before the Romans came the early Britons had begun it; Caesar's legions built a town upon its site, and the lengthening centuries had enlarged and ornamented it. Against its gates the army of Charles I had battered in vain as it sustained the Puritan cause in the west. Not far away is the sleeping little village where William Tyndale was born. In Gloucester rises the beautiful cathedral whose structure goes back to Norman times and ultimately perhaps still further. In the very shadow of that cathedral, of which he was the bishop, John Hooper was burned at the stake in Mary's reign, on a February day of 1555, rather than renounce his Protestant faith. Down one of the old streets still stands the frame house of Robert Raikes who, ten years after

Whitefield's death, organized the first Sunday school in the world. And in that historic old town with its memories of Britons, Romans, Normans, the heroism of the Civil Wars, the martyrdom that marked the Reformation, is the good old English tavern known as the Bell Inn (just such a place as Dickens would have peopled with Victorian immortals), in which on the sixteenth day of December, 1714, George Whitefield was born, of parents who kept the tavern. He was fortunate in his birthplace, because in Gloucester was one of the few schools in England where, two hundred years ago, poor boys could secure anything of an education; but he left the school in his fourteenth year to go to work; and he worked in his mother's tavern—his father being dead by that time—for the most part in what once we called the barroom and for which probably will find no better name in days to come, becoming, as he said, a common drawer, the man who drew the liquor for the patrons—the bartender in our own language, a curious beginning for an evangelistic career.

One day a young fellow of the town, who had gone to Oxford University in spite of poverty and was working his way through as a servitor, waiting on tables for the other and for the most part wealthy students, returned for a visit. He called on his friends at the tavern and reported that he had completed a university term and met all his expenses and had one penny left over. Whitefield's mother—no ordinary character though in ordinary life—turned to young George and asked if he would like to go to Oxford. He said that he would, with all his heart; and so he went.

These pages would become altogether too numerous if they were to follow him through the hard, torturous years of work, of extravagant piety, of his ill-advised and self-inflicted hardships, or of his fellowship with the Wesleys and the Holy Club there, all so much older than he. But let the time pass swiftly and disclose him some years later, six months past twenty-one years of age, in Gloucester for a few months, struggling and praying against ordination, though called to preach, until the wise Bishop of Gloucester sends for him and tells him he should now be ordained. He was ordained; and on the following Sunday, in the Church of Saint Mary, in the city where his mother kept the tavern and he had drawn liquor for the patrons, he preached his first sermon to a congregation that crowded the building. When it was ended, a city knew that no ordinary boy parson, but a strange new prophet had risen. Complaint was made to the Bishop that the young preacher's sermon had driven fifteen people mad. And the Bishop expressed the hope that such madness would remain. It was but a prelude to the extraordinary demonstrations which followed his utterances down the years. He was called to London, a few months later, to preach in the Tower, and though only twenty-two, crowds soon followed him on the streets and it became necessary for him to travel in a closed carriage in order not to stop all traffic. He preached in Bristol within the year; and in the church in Bristol there is still preserved the solemn record that on the occasion of his first sermon there three people in the congregation dropped dead.

While Whitefield was sweeping on toward his tremendous fame, John Wesley was in Georgia trying, against great odds and with the wrong kind of an outlook, to lead the religious life of the new Colony which he was so soon to leave. But while there he wrote Whitefield telling him of the need and urging him to come to America. "Do you ask what you shall have?" Wesley wrote to him. "Food to eat, and raiment to put on, a house to lay your head in, such as your Lord had not; and a crown of glory that fadeth not away." And on those terms Whitefield, twenty-four years old, sailed from England as Wesley, disappointed and a failure in America, returned.

To retell in detail the story of Whitefield's remarkable career would contribute little of significance to the purpose of this chapter. What is significant here is Whitefield and that portion of his career during which he initiated the impact of Methodism upon the New-England theology. For it was the impact of Methodism which he initiated, although theologically Whitefield was far removed from John Wesley, and Whitefield's Methodism long since passed. Having glimpsed the man it will be profitable to trace hurriedly the contribution which he made to American religious life, fitting into the march and movement of religious thought from that austere New England of the

Puritans and Jonathan Edwards down to our own day. With this purpose in view, no attempt is made to distinguish Whitefield's various voyages to America. He crossed the Atlantic thirteen times between 1738, his first, and 1769, his last voyage; and that in a time when ships were incredibly small and at the mercy of the tempests, and the sea was infested by privateers and harried by wars in which neutrals had nothing to expect but piracy. His longest voyage took eleven weeks where now we take five days; his shortest, when, as he said, he was on a fast boat, took twenty-eight days. He stayed only a few months, the first time, returning shortly after a stay in England. Putting his career briefly, it is that at the age when present-day young preachers are either in the theological schools or out upon their first and most inconspicuous charges, Whitefield was an alumnus of Oxford University and held its degree, had preached in the greatest pulpits of England, and was already the center of a popularity no preacher has ever known before or since his day. This is the man, of whose preaching and manners a great deal can be said, who is again in America in 1740, whose chief responsibility is the founding of an orphanage in Savannah, to be built after the manner of a great orphanage in Halle, Germany. On five hundred acres of land given him, he laid the first bricks of the first building, in the spring of 1740, and called it Bethesda because of his hope that it would be a house of mercy to many souls. Then he started northward to raise money for the new institution.

En route, his preaching was marked by the crowds, the demonstrations and the tumultuous conversions of men and women by the hundreds, with by-products which still remain, one of them being Princeton Theological Seminary; Nassau Hall having been inspired through Whitefield's preaching, in recognition of which Methodists in England gave it money and it conferred on Whitefield one of its first Master of Arts degrees. So in the year 1740 he comes into New England, his fame preceding him, and his welcome sure.

I

By 1740 the Great Awakening which had begun in 1734 with Jonathan Edwards's preaching of the absolute and awful sovereignty of God and his unrelieved enmity to men, had been an exhausted movement for almost four years. There had been, as has been observed in the former chapter, an unprecedented revival throughout the colonies, marked by physical excesses, suicides among adults, extravagant and artificial moods forced upon children; and in spite of the grim doctrine that God's inaccessible, undiscoverable will chose the few to salvation and the many to torment, by a curious paradox, conversion had been the very center of the movement. Men and women, and, so it was testified, little children, were converted like Jonathan Edwards himself to the inscrutable sovereignty of God, and many, doubtless, like Edwards himself, felt a sense of profound happiness in their assurance. But the movement ended almost as abruptly as it had begun, its force apparently ended like a spent bullet.

For this, as far as a specific reason can be discovered, one has to look back to the New-England theology against which Edwards lifted his quiet but tremendous voice in protest, a theology given its later shape and direction and established by a man who, in one of the curious coincidences of history, was by blood and theology the last man with whom Edwards would wish to differ. The early New-England theory of the Church was that only Christians of evident and tested faith who were themselves conscious of the power of God in their lives could enter the covenant by which a local church was constituted. Here, again, in that thought of being conscious of the power of God in personal experience can be seen how much better than his conception of God the Calvinist was in his personal character. But the theory also held that just as God's covenant with Abraham included his descendants, so the covenant of Christians which constituted the local church included their children; and as a result there were two ways of entering the Church—by confession of faith and by being born of those who had confessed the faith. But again something was interjected by time and inquiry. What about those who were the children of such tested Christians and had come into the Church and baptism by birth, but who, grown to maturity, had no consciousness of the power of God in their own lives? Were they still members of the Church and, if so, could not their children also be baptized and enter the Church? and if they were not members of the Church, when did they cease to be?

As early as 1639 Richard Mather, the great Puritan preacher of his time, had written the authoritative policy that the children of those who were in the Church by birth and not by confession of faith were themselves not in the Church and could not be baptized; but six years later he changed his mind and argued that as the parents had been born in the Covenant and had never been cast out, their children were such also. Down the succeeding years there were councils and debates and conventions concerning it; there were books and tracts written in the controversy; and there was a division in New England churches over what was called the Half-way Covenant, by which it was laid down that those who were in the church by reason of their parents' covenant, were themselves members even if they were not conscious of any work of grace within their hearts, and their children could be baptized as members, but they themselves could not be admitted to the Lord's Supper or to a vote in the church affairs. By the year 1700 this system was general throughout New England, and had been further developed in many places to the teaching that these men and women who had come into the Church as children by reason of their parents' religious experience, were sufficiently church members, because of the promise of God to Abraham "to be a God unto thee, and to thy seed after thee," to come to the Lord's Supper also, and that it was their duty so to do. The man who established this system of thought in the upper Connecticut Valley and gave it an impetus elsewhere was Jonathan Edwards's grandfather and predecessor, and he himself preached for twenty years in Northampton without disturbing the practice, although his preaching for many of those years was a criticism of it.

Logically, the half-Covenant was inevitable, and Solomon Stoddard was correct in his thinking as Richard Mather had been before him; for if the Calvinistic premise is accepted, that God ordains to everlasting life those whom He elects for no merit of their own, and ordains to everlasting torment those whom He rejects for no evil they have done but out of His arbitrary inscrutable will and for His own greater glory, then men and women who assent intellectually to the belief, though they have no experience or sense of any work of God within them, have right to all the ordinances of religion because, even so, they may be of the elect. And against that firm and bulwarked theology the fervor of a revival which in practice contradicted it, must at last go down. It did go down, with the swift fading of the movement, two years after its beginning, and in 1740 there was little of the great tempest which had so recently swept the colonies except the memories it had left and many relapses from the quickening which multitudes had felt.

Then George Whitefield came to New England, leaving behind him, from Savannah northward, a trail of blazing religious passion, and flinging before him the unprecedented fame which had crossed the Atlantic from his triumphs in England and was already being vindicated on this side of the sea. He was twenty-six years old; and it is difficult to imagine those staid New Englanders greeting him as they did. Several miles from Boston he was met by a procession led by the governor's son, and escorted through the city. Most of the ministers were cordial, though one was not. He met Whitefield on the street and said, "I am sorry to see you here." "So is the devil," said Whitefield; and that was that. He preached at Harvard College and revolutionized for a time its social life. He preached under the tree where thirty-five years later Washington took command of the Revolutionary armies. The governor of the state personally conveyed him to some of his appointments. In the eighteen months he was in New England more than thirty religious societies were organized as a result of his preaching; and the Great Awakening which had died away in 1736 was now blazing more widely than ever. He preached four times for Jonathan Edwards, and the revival which followed him, once more carried on by Edwards afterward, continued for another two years.

But the picture is not all in bright colors. He was only twenty-six, and he made mistakes. He was foolish in some public criticisms; he was sometimes unwise in his personal utterances; and he permitted his diary to be printed with some very unkind and indiscreet strictures on persons and churches. When he left, he was to return again, but never to the welcome and never to the undivided enthusiasm which he had at this time and lost.

What enabled him to fit into New England in so compelling a fashion and rekindle the fire which had died under the direction of Jonathan Edwards was, first, his theology; and, second, his inconsistency; and then that supreme, unprecedented gift of his as the greatest preacher, the most compelling voice that as yet had proclaimed the gospel in England or America. As for his theology, he was a Calvinist; and while it is no part of this chapter, it is to be remembered in passing that Whitefield and the Wesleys soon parted, with some bitterness on his part, because he was a Calvinist, though later they were genuinely reunited in personal affection; and from him though not by him came the branch of Methodism which, never strong, has practically perished, the Calvinistic Methodists. So, theologically, he was agreeable to the New-England clergy and their churches. His inconsistencies gave a new power to his evangelistic preaching which the sterner and more terrible consistency of Edwards could not permanently command. Whitefield argued that while God elects arbitrarily those whom He will save, no one knows the elect from the others, and so he could honestly offer salvation to all who accept it; and with his illogical mind, he thus offered a universal gospel. He preached, it is true, on the terrible nature of sin and the terrors of hell and the helplessness of men; but he preached also of the emptiness of a life without Christ, the joy of Christlike living, and the all-sufficiency of Christ as the Saviour of the world. Men and women forgot the contradiction between his gospel and his theology and theirs, and multitudes were converted. So the Great Awakening was revived and re-empowered.

II

It has already been remarked that his was the most compelling voice that had proclaimed the gospel in England or America. What was it, and what sort of preacher was he? He was physically very animated, yet produced few of the more dramatic extravagances of John Wesley's preaching. But he was an artist, an actor with everything which goes to constitute the undefinable quality of genius. Illustrations, perhaps, will be better than description.

His itinerating northward from Savannah and the seat of his Bethesda orphanage, as has been remarked, was to secure funds for the project as well as to preach an evangelistic gospel to the New World; and we may begin to judge him as a preacher by the way men responded to his appeals. He knew nothing of organizing campaigns, appointing team captains and following up with a card index system and a series of pledges. He did business on a cash basis, and Benjamin Franklin may be accepted as an unprejudiced witness. Franklin was two years younger than Whitefield and was publishing the *Pennsylvania Gazette* in Philadelphia when Whitefield came the first time. He wrote of Whitefield's preaching, in 1740, that enormous crowds of all sects and denominations attended his services and that it was a matter of speculation for himself to observe the

> extraordinary influence of his oratory on his hearers, and how much they admired and respected him notwithstanding his common abuse of them, by assuring them that they were naturally half beasts and half devils. It was wonderful to see the change made in the manners of our inhabitants. From being thoughtless and indifferent about religion, it seemed as if all the world were growing religious, so that one could not walk through Philadelphia in the morning without hearing psalms sung in different families on every street.

Franklin made a series of tests while Whitefield was preaching from the Courthouse steps and estimated that he could be heard by a congregation of more than thirty thousand, so loud and clear and penetrating was his voice. He was preaching on the Courthouse steps one evening, the Courthouse being where the Markethouse now is, near the river, and he was heard on the Delaware side; while sailors in their ships coming up the river could distinguish the words. Franklin was equally impressed with the skill with which Whitefield moved congregations to give money for his orphanage. His own testimony is worth rereading:

> His eloquence had wonderful power over the hearts

and purses of his hearers, of which I myself was an instance. I did not disapprove of the design; but, as Georgia was then destitute of materials and workmen, and it was proposed to send them from Philadelphia at great expense, I thought it would have been better to have built the house at Philadelphia, and to have brought the children to it. This I advised; but he was resolute in his first project, and rejected my counsel; and I, therefore, refused to contribute. I happened some time after to attend one of his sermons, in the course of which I perceived he intended to finish with a collection; and I silently resolved he should get nothing from me. I had in my pocket a handful of copper money, three or four silver dollars, and five pistoles of gold. As he proceeded I began to soften, and concluded to give the copper. Another stroke of his oratory determined me to give the silver; and he finished so admirably that I emptied my pocket wholly into the collection dish, gold and all. At this sermon there was also one of our Club, who, being of my sentiments respecting the building in Georgia, and suspecting a collection might be intended, emptied his pocket before he came from home. Toward the conclusion of the discourse, however, he felt a strong inclination to give, and applied to a neighbor who stood near him, to lend him money for the purpose. The request was fortunately made to, perhaps, the only man in the company who had firmness not to be affected by the preacher. His answer was, "At any other time, friend Hopkinson, I would lend thee freely, but not now, for thee seems to be out of thy right senses."

In one collection in Boston he received more than five thousand dollars. It was in Boston, also, that a member of the Harvard faculty known as Old Father Flynt, who was well known for the ability with which he kept his generous impulses in restraint, went to hear Whitefield preach. He was so moved by the sheer eloquence of the man that when the collection was taken he took almost automatically a large bill from his pocket and dropped it in the plate. He was sullen and silent all the way home afterward, and when a student asked him how he liked Whitefield, he thundered, "Like him! why the dog has robbed me of a five-pound note."

But his great and moving results were not for the most part in getting men's money; they were in moving their imaginations and minds and feelings until they surrendered to the Christ whom he proclaimed. He vivified every scene. Preaching by the East River in New York City, one day, to a crowd, largely of sailors, he began with a picture of them sailing over a smooth sea under a cloudless sky, then described in short, swift words a rising storm, then the beat of the tempests, the breaking of the ship, and cried, "What next?" As he paused for an instant, one of the sailors, wholly forgetting everything except the emotion of the moment, shouted, "Take to the long-boat, sir!" and then Whitefield drove home his gospel of salvation. David Garrick said that he would give a hundred guineas if he could say "Oh!" like Mr. Whitefield. He took advantage of passing events to the extent that he sometimes carried with him a black cap such as was worn by judges when they pronounced sentence of death, and when he was in a town where a criminal had recently been sentenced or executed, in the course of his sermon, which was appropriate, he would put on the black cap and then, enacting the part, pronounce sentence of death on the sinner. Preaching one day in the open air, a thunderstorm swept overhead, and Whitefield made every feature of it from the crashing thunder and the lightning to the later outbreak of the sun and the rainbow serve his turn. Afterward friends requested a copy of the sermon for publication and he replied, "I have no objection if you will print the lightning, thunder, and rainbow with it."

A well-known shipbuilder was so prejudiced against him that he refused even to hear him but was persuaded to go just once. At the close of the sermon someone asked him what he thought of Whitefield. "Think!" he said, "I never heard such a man in my life. I tell you, sir, every Sunday when I go to church, I can build a ship from stem to stern under the sermon; but, were it to save my soul, under Mr. Whitefield, I could not lay a single plank." In England there was no more famous scoffer than Lord Chesterfield. He was listening to Whitefield one day comparing the sinner to a blind man on a dangerous road, when his dog that led him had gotten away and the blind man is exploring with his stick the road that skirts a cliff. On the edge of the cliff the stick slips from his fingers and falls into the abyss; and all unconscious of his peril the blind man stoops to pick it up, and stumbles—and so vivid was Whitefield's manner that Lord Chesterfield jumped to his feet with the shout, "Good God, he's gone!"

This was the man who returned one Saturday evening from Portsmouth to the home of a friend in Newburyport, so ill that after an early supper he excused himself and went to his room to rest, having already said that his sun was about to set. But the news spread that he was back in town and a crowd gathered in front of the house, filled the rooms and begged that he would give them at least a brief exhortation. So, standing on the stairs, with a candle in his hand, he spoke his last gospel message and with great difficulty lay down, but not to sleep; and just after dawn came in upon the New England that he loved, for him the day broke and all shadows fled away. He was only fifty-six years old and had been famous for one supreme gift only, for thirty-five of these years. Today nothing remains but his name, a few sermons which do not even suggest his power, a simple hardly-visited monument or two. He organized no society, he founded no denomination, he administered no churches, he wrote no theology. He was, like John the Baptist, a voice preparing the way of the Lord. But he made a permanent contribution to American religious history and life and we are his inheritors.

III

It is apparent, even from so sketchy a discussion as the limits of this volume make inevitable, that Whitefield greatly strengthened that New-

England theology over which the name of Jonathan Edwards was to cast its shadow for a century. For Whitefield's extraordinary gift of eloquence by which to move men and women deeply, that strange, evanescent magnetism which made him the center not of interest alone, but of violent and vocal enthusiasm—something Jonathan Edwards never had—all of that went to the support of the theology of predestination and the rigid, absolute, unchangeable sovereignty of God. To the logic of Edwards and the older Puritan preachers Whitefield added a passion. He woke the confidence of stirred emotions and evoked the stormy certainties of deep and precious though mysterious constraints. This is of more than biographical interest, for in matters of religious experience it is only the few who keep in sight the cogencies of reason; the multitudes are moved and held and established by unthought immediacies of feeling; and who is wise enough to say that they are wrong? "There are certain truths," someone has written, "and these the highest, that only open to the pure in heart. You cannot see them with the mind till the soul gets there."[1] So that while the gospel and the experience which Whitefield preached were quite in contradiction to the theology of predestination which he claimed, nevertheless the reality of the experience in the lives of men and women carried with it, in their minds, an acceptance of the theology with which it was illogi-

[1] Brierly: *Religion and Today,* p. 85.

cally identified; and the New-England theology, the Calvinism of the Puritans, came down the years strengthened and re-enforced in popular life by Whitefield as much as it was renewed in the higher regions of thought by Jonathan Edwards.

But real as that service was, it was by no means the greatest which Whitefield accomplished. He prepared the way in a remarkable degree for historic Methodism which was so soon to have such a notable career in the New World. Whitefield was a Calvinist in theology but he was a Methodist in life, experience, and in what today would be called technique. He was associated with the Wesleys in their work in England, and though theologically differing from them, in affection, regard, and co-operation, one with them, except for a very short time. It was Whitefield who had brought Wesley to Bristol and against his will practically forced on him the field preaching which became the very power of Methodism in its beginnings. It was Whitefield at first, more than the Wesleys, who popularized the new movements in British church life. Like the Wesleys he was a member and a clergyman of the Church of England and never ceased to be so. And when, after his thirty years of preaching in America, after the colonies from Georgia to Massachusetts for a generation had been accustomed to the impassioned evangelism of Whitefield calling men and women to repentance and faith, those first Methodist preachers came—Francis Asbury, the leader of them all, Jesse Lee with his special mission in New

England—preaching with no such eloquence but with the same fire, the same passion, the same certainty, the same lucid insight into the heart of man, those Methodist preachers found a preparation for them which has by no means been sufficiently recognized by history. The Methodists were the exact antagonists theologically of the New Englanders from the Pilgrim Fathers down to Jonathan Edwards. Instead of the arbitrary and absolute sovereignty of God choosing some, rejecting others for His own glory, they proclaimed the free will of men enabled to determine their own destiny by an act of choice and a direction of the will. Instead of a salvation limited by the inscrutable will of God to a few, they declared a salvation that was actually and not simply in theory, as Whitefield had it, for every one. "Whosoever will," they said, "may take of the water of life freely." Instead of the New-England and Calvinist doctrine that God was in enmity with the race, they preached that God was a God of love and that the death of Christ was to reconcile not God to men but men to God. They came bringing overseas the conflict between two theologies which had been at war in Europe since a Dutch theologian, in 1629, had faced the triumphant contemporary Calvinism of the Divine Decrees and limited salvation, with the Arminianism that claimed free grace and preached a God who, like a father, desired the salvation of all the children of men. And Whitefield, holding the one theology and preaching the other experience, unintentionally made a broad highway in the minds and hearts of the eighteenth and nineteenth centuries for the Methodists and their gospel in which theology and experience coincided in a conviction of the universal love of God. It is that, of course, which now holds the field. The sons of the Puritans, the theological children of Jonathan Edwards, and the spiritual descendants of the Wesleys now preach and believe and pray and live alike in one common faith and practice; and it was historically over George Whitefield as a bridge that in America they have united.

And, finally, George Whitefield has put religious men and women in his debt, and our own generation has no greater need than to recover this inheritance, by his bequest of the fact and the demonstration of it that more than our natural energies are waiting for us in the struggles and achievements of the spiritual life; that there are more things not alone in prayer but in the whole religious life than our philosophy has dreamed of, and that one may adventure, must adventure, upon the unseen, unexplained mysteries of God if he is to be all that he hopes and wants to be. It was one of the solemn utterances of Doctor Jowett that "it is impossible to meet with a single unconverted man who does not know that, if ever he is to wear the glory of the Son of God, and to be chaste and illumined in his most hidden thoughts and dispositions, there will have to take place some marvelous and inconceivable transformation."[2] In

[2] Jowett: *The Epistles of St. Peter*, p. 5.

our day of moral discipline on the one hand, and moral relaxation on the other; of religious education here and religious skepticism yonder; of fanatic trust in the operations of natural science to produce perfect humanity, and a shallow feeling that humanity cannot be perfected at all; in this day, nothing is more needed than a recovery of the truth which Whitefield so illustrated and empowered—that supernatural forces can be tapped for human regeneration and that God is a present help on whom men may adventure. The witness to the credibility of all that they have hoped and dreamed of God making them what they cannot make of themselves, is in the historic Jesus become the Christ of faith.

References

Belden, A. D., *George Whitefield—the Awakener.*

Belcher, Joseph, *George Whitefield.*

Davenport, F. M., *Primitive Traits in Religious Revivals.*

Gillies, John, *Memoirs of the Life and Character of the Rev. George Whitefield, A.M.*

Hall, Thomas C., *The Religious Background of American Culture.*

North, Eric M., *Early Methodist Philanthropy.*

Tyerman, Luke, *The Life of the Rev. George Whitefield,* two volumes.

IV

METHODIST ITINERANTS: CREATORS OF CLIMATE

IV

METHODIST ITINERANTS: CREATORS OF CLIMATE

THOMAS WENTWORTH HIGGINSON, in one of the entries in his *Journal* for 1852, quotes a friend as saying that "Every New Englander looks as if he were just stopping here a minute on his way to parts unknown." It may have been only a passing remark with no more substantial basis than humorous fancy, but it is singularly descriptive of the Methodist preachers whose coming to New England in the path of George Whitefield was mentioned in the preceding chapter. That was not to be until nineteen years after Whitefield's death, when Jesse Lee reached Norwalk, Connecticut, on the twentieth of June, 1789, and one woman having refused him permission to preach in a house and another forbidden him to stand in her orchard, he addressed himself to some twenty people who gathered around him on the street. "When he was done," a spectator reported later, "and we had an opportunity of expressing our views to each other, it was agreed that such a man had not visited New England since the days of Whitefield. I heard him again, and thought I could follow him to the ends of the earth."[1] At the time Jesse Lee

[1] Memoir of Rev. T. Ware, quoted in Leroy M. Lee: *Life and Times of Jesse Lee,* 221f.; also Stevens: *History of the Methodist Episcopal Church,* 2, p. 404f.

was the only Methodist in all New England. Eighteen years later, when he revisited New England for the last time, there were eleven thousand Methodists, organized in classes, churches, circuits, districts and Conferences. Francis Asbury had again and again traveled its towns, cities, and countrysides, as his *Journal* and that of Lee record.

The Methodists came to New England as to a land in spiritual need. The old order was changing rapidly, and while they have left no records to indicate any appreciation of the new ways of thought and life, the facts are clear, and it is not difficult to believe that minds as shrewd as theirs recognized them.

> The principles of liberty, the right of men to happiness and representative government, which nourished the zeal of the American patriots in their struggle with England and shaped the ideals of the newly freed country, had already made the theology of Calvinism irrelevant to the social thought-patterns of the period.[2]

It was not, however, the irrelevance of Calvinism which challenged the Methodists; it was the sterility in personal religious life which they saw was compatible with its theology. They did not underestimate its intellectual distinction. To the contrary, while opposing its theological errors and seeking to make good its spiritual failure, they acknowledged the disciplines of mind and conduct which it wrought:

---

[2] Haroutunian: *Piety Versus Moralism,* p. 177.

The cross, with its subduing and transforming influences, was removed from its position in the system of redemption; and instead of concentrating the heart with its affections, the soul with its hopes, upon Christ —the only Saviour of sinners—the pulpit sought to employ the mind with a dull and endless speculation upon eternal prescience, and the omnipotence of divine decrees. The effect of such a system of religious training might have been easily foreseen. The habit of considering doctrines so abstruse and intricate cannot fail to enlarge and strengthen the intellect. And, when superadded to even the common-school system of education, it will contribute very materially to the social rectitude and moral integrity of a people. Such was the character of the New-England states, at the period of their history now passing under review. The people were of grave and orderly deportment, of an inquisitive turn of mind, fond of controversy—especially upon religious subjects —strict observers of the Sabbath, and devoted to their ecclesiastical government, their modes of faith, and forms of worship.[3]

New England was peculiarly proud of and loyal to its colleges. But the colleges, whatever services they rendered the intelligence of the time, did nothing for its moral character. The Rev. Dr. Ezra Stiles, president of Yale for seventeen years during which the religious life of the college steadily deteriorated, indicated the helplessness of the "liberalism" which he represented when, in a sermon some five years after his installation, he said, "Here deism will have its full chance; nor need libertines more to complain of being over-

[3] Lee: *Life and Times of the Rev. Jesse Lee,* p. 220.

come by any weapons but the gentle, the powerful ones of argument and truth." Dr. William Warren Sweet, in his Drew Lectures, puts beside that utterance of the president of Yale, the observation of Lyman Beecher, who became a student there before Doctor Stiles left:

> College was in a most ungodly state. The college church was almost extinct. Most of the students were skeptical, and rowdies were plenty. Wines and liquors were kept in many rooms; intemperance, profanity, gambling, and licentiousness were common.

It is only fair to New England to add that like conditions prevailed in colleges elsewhere. Secular affairs in the New-England states, as contemporary historians report, flourished but spiritual conditions had grown seriously worse. The influence of Tom Paine was registered in increasing infidelity. "Great looseness of manners and morals had replaced the ancient Puritanic strictness." "The profanation of the Sabbath," said Timothy Dwight in 1801, "before unusual, profaneness of language, drunkenness, gambling, and lewdness, were exceedingly increased."

What, however, roused the crusading passion of the Methodists, perhaps more strongly than anything else, was the absence from the lives of the orthodox Christians of that vital and creative personal experience which, as Wesleyans, they identified with conversion; belief in which was not a factor in New-England faith. One of the foremost critics of Whitefield's preaching had declared that "conversion does not appear alike necessary for ministers in their private capacity."[4] Regeneration was considered "not ascertainable by investigation, and not necessary to church membership or the ministerial office!"[5] The experience with which Methodism is most distinctly identified, that of the knowledge of the forgiveness of sin, New England denounced as heretical presumption. No less a person than Jonathan Edwards defended himself from the suspicion that his "assurance of faith," implied it.

Holding convictions at such variance from the views of New-England orthodoxy, the Methodist preachers found the theological climate particularly cold, but no colder than the social weather which they encountered. Jesse Lee's *Journal,* like the journals of his colleagues everywhere, is a vivid picture of perseverance which only an overwhelming commitment of duty could sustain. He preached on a certain very cold and wintry Christmas Eve, and then recorded in his *Journal:* "To-night, thanks be to God, I was invited by a widow woman to put up at her house. This is the first invitation I have had since I first came to the place, which is between six and seven months." Repulsed again and again, meeting discourtesy on every hand, insult often and abuse not infrequently, the Methodist preachers nevertheless persisted. While they were primarily concerned

[4] Stevens: *History of the Methodist Episcopal Church,* Vol. II, p. 408.
[5] *Ibid.,* p. 407.

for the practical life and experience of the people, they recognized in the doctrines of Calvinism the deep-lying causes of New England's dearth of vigorous religious experience. Their sermons consequently were not only invitations to repentance and expositions of their distinctive doctrine of the witness of the Spirit; they were a practical apologetic for Arminianism, over its whole range of Free Will, Growth in Grace, Christian Perfection, the possibility of a Christian's falling from grace—the entire body of doctrines against which Calvinism had fought from the beginning, and to which New England was peculiarly hostile.

The story of Methodism in New England is a story, therefore, not only of intellectual controversy but, as elsewhere, of physical hardships, personal sacrifice and suffering, social humiliation, and public abuse, endured by intrepid men whose "enthusiasm" has been recognized with contempt on the part of opponents and honor by fellow evangelicals, but whose intellectual gifts and discriminating theological minds have seldom been fully appreciated. The Methodists were to be recognized by qualities of conduct and life, but it was life that took its direction from an experience which had been evoked by the confident acceptance of clearly articulated doctrines of faith. Their theology interpreted their experience.

But Methodism, in its creative stage in New England, cannot be set before us in the sketch of any one preacher. For its preachers were not settled in a community so as to gather around themselves, and so become the representatives of, the current movements of life and thought. They were itinerants constantly on the road. They preached almost daily and in a different place each time. Slowly, of course, there came the establishment of fixed pastorates, but even then, the preacher remained on the same circuit, and later the "station," for only a year or two at the most. Even this to us normal and desirable evolution was resented by the pioneers. As early as 1813, twenty-four years after Jesse Lee first came, Francis Asbury, during one of his visits throughout New England, wrote in his *Journal:* "I have difficulties to encounter, but I must be silent. My mind is in God. In New England we sing, we build houses, we eat, and stand at prayer. Here preachers locate, and people support them, and have traveling preachers also. Were I to labor forty-two years more, I suppose I should not succeed in getting things right. Preachers have been sent away from Newport by an apostate; so we go. O rare steeple-houses, bells (organs by and by?)—these things are against me, and contrary to the simplicity of Christ."

Bishop Asbury might disapprove of the way in which Methodism developed in New England, but at heart there was no difference between him and his colleagues in their convictions on the essentials of faith and life.

The texts from which Jesse Lee preached on his first invasion of New England, as reported in his biography by Leroy M. Lee, are revealing:

John 3. 7:—Ye must be born again.
Romans 6. 23:—For the wages of sin is death, but the gift of God is eternal life, through Jesus Christ our Lord.
Amos 5. 6:—Seek ye the Lord, and ye shall live.
Isaiah 55. 6:—Seek ye the Lord while he may be found, call ye.
John 10. 27:—My sheep hear my voice, and I know them, and they follow me.
Ephesians 5. 1:—Be ye followers of God as dear children.
Matthew 22. 14:—For many are called, but few are chosen.

His biographer enlarged on this sermon, the text of which lent itself so thoroughly to Calvinism's doctrine of election.

On this occasion he had an unusually large number of hearers, and among them two ministers—a Baptist and a Congregationalist, the former sitting at his side, the other just before him. Under these circumstances he stated and defended these propositions as the doctrine of the text: I. That all men are called to forsake their sins. II. That with this call, the gracious power of obedience is given to the sinner. And III. That men are called before they are chosen. This was a point-blank shot at Calvinism and took effect in the very center of its creed.[6]

Job 22. 21.—Acquaint now thyself with Him, and be at peace, etc.
Mark 8. 36:—For what shall it profit a man, if he shall gain the whole world, and lose his own soul?
John 5. 40:—And ye will not come to me, that ye might have life.

---

[6] Lee: *Life and Times of the Rev. Jesse Lee,* pp. 228, 229.

Asbury's *Journal* discloses the same sort of scriptural basis for his preaching, as do the sermons of the other Methodist itinerants.

The Methodist preachers, quite apart from their theology and the hardships they encountered in proclaiming it, deserve in themselves far more than a passing reference. If they could not measure up to Macaulay's famous tribute to the English Puritans whose representative was John Milton, as "the most remarkable body of men, perhaps, which the world has ever produced," they were nevertheless a remarkable body of men. There were some very able and intellectually trained men among them. Jesse Lee, after Whitefield, the leader of the Methodist invasion of New England, wrote the first history of the Methodist Church, had the reputation of being the ablest preacher in the connection, and for six years was chaplain of the United States House of Representatives, resigning the office the year before his death. Much of their essential greatness, the accuracy of their insights, the shrewd, disciplined genius of their minds, has been overlooked because their influence went into personal lives rather than into literature. They wrote few books and did not publish their sermons. There were diversities of gifts among them. They were men with individuality, and idiosyncrasies were part of their character. They had the substance of effective education and were at home in the theological controversies of the times, but no school, committed to a fixed theological method and literary standard, had cast their native abilities into a conventional form. Their varied and personal talents had freedom of range. Their judgments, their sympathies, and their insights were hampered by no standardized conventionality of appeal. As a result, they were effective propagandists, and they could hardly have been effective had they been less than versatile, for they had to capture not only trained minds in their audiences but the untrained and illiterate; and personal manner went as far in convincing utterance as theological presentation and rhetorical eloquence. They were of that gifted type of men who, whether Lollard preachers in the fourteenth century or pack-men and peddlers in every century since, have immediate access into popular favor by reason of their sheerly human qualities of sympathy, understanding, and humor.

They were, all alike, the inheritors of a definite tradition. Much has been said, and little more needs be said, of the spiritual decay into which English society had fallen in the eighteenth century to which Wesley came, both nonconformist and that which remained loyal to the Established Church. The most eloquent and uncompromising testimony to that decay has been given by clergymen of the Church itself—Bishop Burnet, Archbishop Secker, Robert Southey the poet, and notable others. Even deeper than that as a factor in the reception which the eighteenth century gave to the Methodists was the fact that Established theology and the beliefs of Calvinism alike had no principle of personal assurance. There was the

New Testament, there were the Thirty-nine Articles, the Prayer Book, the Westminster Confession, the Sacraments; one could subscribe to them and participate in their use. But salvation was a mystery, and who could say who would be saved? Who could declare the elect? One could only hope that good would be the final goal of ill.

Into that generation burst the ranting Methodists of England with their revolutionary evangel that men and women could know that they were saved. To the Establishment they declared that one need not grope and cling to a great tradition and the magic of a rite; but that in his heart was waiting to be summoned a witness more sure and unmistakable than absolution. To the Calvinist they thundered that God's inscrutable decrees were not concealed in the dark of a distant Judgment Day, but were already to be recognized in the Covenant written within the heart. And the tumult of such a gospel, proclaimed defiantly and triumphantly by masons and tanners and colliers and the like unlearned and ill-bred men, led by a few mad clergy who had forgotten the dignity of the altar, battered at the pride and culture of Churchmen and conforming laity, and their first rejoinder was denial and then suppression by abuse.

American Methodists in the late eighteenth and early nineteenth centuries had inherited all that is involved in the circumstances that historic Methodism began in such a revolt from conformity. From the beginning it conformed to its tradition of revolt. It swept through its world in a break from established precedent, and its own precedents of difference have created for it the custom of irregularity. From its beginning Methodism has been a constitution of paradox. It has always been charged with being dogmatic; but while it has several doctrines its only dogma is freedom of belief. Criticized as ignorant, it was born in a university, and since 1775 has inspired, originated, and maintained more institutions of higher learning than any other body. Condemned as narrow, it admits without hesitation members from all other churches that exalt Christ, and dismisses its members to all others without embarrassment. It administers baptism in all forms, joins with the historic episcopate in the laying on of hands, allies itself with Independency through its Quarterly Conferences and its responsibility of laymen for all licenses to preach; keeps step with Calvinism by its conviction of the providence of God; can sympathize with Rome in its emphasis upon the supernatural character of Redemption, and matches the Quakers' Inner Light with its own Witness of the Spirit. It welcomes the most revolutionary disclosures of science and criticism, for its God is the God of the living, and it remembers the years at the right hand of the Most High, in which truth will prevail. Social propaganda does not frighten it, for in the very beginning it joined individual conversion and social reform. Politicians dislike it and it returns the compliment, but they do now awe it; for its sons have ornamented Parliaments and sat in Presidential chairs; its daughters have married princes, its ambassadors have stood before kings. Confident of another world, it is at home in this. The march of armies and the menace of governments do not alarm it, for its mission is to all nations and it knows them to be no more than men. The confusions of mind which darken judgment and deceive hope do not shake its certainties, for its only permanence is readiness to change.

The mistreatment which the Methodist preachers received in New England does not make pleasant reading, but in fairness to New Englanders it has to be remembered that this Wesleyan tradition, the very strength of the Methodists' devotion, the personal fervor of their religious experience, made it almost inevitable that they should give considerable irritation to disagreeing minds. Human nature is so constituted that any radical piety is likely to be a provocation, and any piety claiming some special treasure is sheer vexation to conventional life. So the prophets are generally stoned and the apostles of any new faith—social or religious—are resented as disturbers of the peace. There are also enough eccentricities of belief engaging the lunatic fringe to make the career of a true prophet the more dangerous.

It is difficult to be radically different without being peculiar; and it is very easy for especially earnest people to believe that they are doing only their duty when they are really minding other people's business. So that the picture of many an old-time Methodist on fire for God looks, at times, uncommonly like a portrait of Meddlesome Mattie. They had strict ideas about their clothing, they were against amusements, they raised very rigid standards for their own domestic and personal life and worship—all of which was well and good; though it was hard on their children. But they could hardly avoid attempting to dispose of other people's affairs in the same way. The annals of early Methodists are not without episodes in which it is difficult to distinguish the line between religious fervor and social frightfulness. They were instant in season and out of season, reproving, rebuking, exhorting, as Saint Paul admonished, but not always with the long-suffering which he counseled at the same time.

Through the stiffer personal qualities which are implied in such a character as this, the Methodist preachers had and instinctively employed the gift of humor which, not always refined, was neither mean nor bitter and had no respect of persons. Two familiar examples are perhaps worth recalling. The secretary of a Conference was calling the roll, one day, while Bishop McKendree presided. "William Hibbard," he called; and there was no response.

"Brother Hibbard," said Bishop McKendree, "why don't you answer to your name?"

"I will," said Brother Hibbard, "when he calls my name."

"Is not your name William?"

"No, Sir."

"What is it?"

"Billy," was the answer.

"Billy!" said the Bishop, with great emphasis. "That is a little boy's name."

"I know it," said this old-time itinerant, "I was a very little boy when my father gave it to me."

Years later, in the westward march of the frontier, a pioneer preacher named Nolley followed some fresh wagon tracks in a distant and lonely part of Missouri, and came upon a settler just unloading his goods and family on a raw homestead, remote from any neighbor. He introduced himself, and the settler made a reply that has become historic.

"Another Methodist preacher!" he said. "I left Virginia for Georgia to get clear of them. There they got my wife and daughter, and I came here, and here is one before I get my wagon unloaded."

"My friend," said the preacher, "if you go to heaven you'll find Methodist preachers there; if you go to hell, I'm afraid you'll find some there; and you see how it is on earth, so you had better make your terms with us and be at peace."

It was this instinctive spontaneous, irrepressible humor of thought and expression, in New England as elsewhere, and down every generation, which has saved the Methodist itinerant amid the monotony and hardships of his life.

Whether truly educated, as was Jesse Lee, or trained only by common sense and piety, the Methodist preachers without much distinction among them were for the most part like the apostles before the Sanhedrin, unlearned and ignorant men when judged by the standards of New England's theological pundits. But their effectiveness was not confined to the unschooled and thoughtless. The annals of New-England Methodism, like its history elsewhere, are bright with brilliant minds which it has won to its convictions of Christian faith and life. For whatever may have been the intellectual qualities of its heralds or their lack of the discipline of the schools; whatever may have been the refinements or crudities of its preachers, they have had a common evangel. Their message was clothed in as many forms as there were messengers, but it was standardized by a common religious experience into a unified proclamation of the free grace of a forgiving God. The divine sovereignty, the providence of God, the pre-eminence of Christ, the universal atonement, and then their own distinctive doctrine, the Witness of the Spirit—these were their common themes; and for them and their evangel, Whitefield's inconsistency had broken a trail. They held a good deal of essential theology in common with Calvinism, but they inferred from it a contradictory sequence. They left Whitefield's inconsistency behind them but carried forward the inclusiveness of his gospel, and through all New England, as elsewhere, they were voices of freedom, hope, and the benignant grace of God, against Calvinistic orthodoxy's inexorable decrees, its desperate uncertainty, and its exalted wrath of God. For the genius of Methodism, as it penetrated New England, precisely that which characterized it elsewhere, was its reference of everything to Christ.

To the new Calvinism, the life of Christ, apart from the agony of the cross, was theologically irrelevant. Christian living became identified with obedience to the moral law of God as revealed to Moses, and the fear of God's vindictive justice was made its foundation. All things revolved around the "moral law." God became the great Enforcer of the moral law, the blood of Christ became the evidence that God will punish transgression. Holy love faded into conformity to the moral law, and such conformity was now the measure and substance of "true virtue."[7]

In sheer contradiction, into every experience, in the face of every forbidding doctrine, the Methodists thrust the figure of Christ, the Son, the Incarnation, the Divine, and said, "Behold the Lamb of God that taketh away the sin of the world." Before His figure, as they presented Him, whether with refinements of language which the intellectual snobbery of New England did not expect, or in all the crudeness of an unlettered lay ministry, speculations dissolved, meticulous dogmas seemed unreal, predestination was but a word. The very spirit of the pioneering Methodist preacher in New England, as in the British Isles and elsewhere in America, is in Charles Wesley's hymn:

"Happy if with my latest breath
  I may but gasp His name;
Preach Him in life and cry in death,
  'Behold, behold, the Lamb!' "

[7] Haroutunian: *Piety Versus Moralism*, p. 176.

And while 11,000 members in the new, crude, poor Methodist churches are not a great numerical result of twenty-four years' work, the changed beliefs and attitudes and feelings in many thousands both of the unchurched and in the orthodox churches, as a consequence of the climate of faith which those eleven thousand generated and sustained, must not be underestimated. It was a climate in which Calvinism could keep alive but did not flourish; and in which liberalism, though no less repugnant to Methodism than to Calvinism itself, found a bracing atmosphere.

References

Baldwin, Alice M., *The New England Clergy and the American Revolution.*

Buckley, James M., *A History of Methodism in the United States.*

Hurst, John Fletcher, *The History of Methodism,* Vol. V.

Lee, Jesse, *A Short History of the Methodists in the United States of America.*

Lee, LeRoy, *The Life and Times of Jesse Lee.*

Luccock, Halford, and Hutchinson, Paul, *The Story of Methodism.*

Stevens, Abel, *Compendious History of American Methodism.*

Stevens, Abel, *History of the Methodist Episcopal Church in the United States,* Vol. III.

Sweet, William W., *Methodism in American History.*

Sweet, William W., *The Story of Religions in America.*

Tipple, Ezra S., *The Heart of Asbury's Journal.*

Ware, Thomas, *Sketches of the Life and Travels of the Rev. Thomas Ware.*

V

WILLIAM ELLERY CHANNING: A THEOLOGICAL HAMLET

V

WILLIAM ELLERY CHANNING: A THEOLOGICAL HAMLET

How effective that other liberalism was to which reference was made at the close of the preceding chapter can be discovered from a contemporary witness. Fifty-three years after Jesse Lee came to New England, twenty-six years after his death, a writer in *The New England Puritan* for September, 1842, said:

> The Unitarian apostasy has involved a large proportion of the churches which were organized by the first settlers of New England. In the Plymouth colony the original churches were first in the apostasy, and the church in South Marshfield is now the oldest Orthodox church in that colony. And, in the Massachusetts colony, the six first in order, of the time of organization, have gone, and the church in Lynn is now the oldest Orthodox church of the Massachusetts colony. All that were established before it have despised their birthright, and are in hostility to the doctrines and religion of the Puritans and of the Reformation.

The story of the New-England theology, however scantily it may be told, must therefore take into account the disintegrating effect not only of that evangelical Protestantism which rejected the extremes of Calvinistic doctrine but also the more radical intellectual movement which denied the central doctrines of all Christian orthodoxy—the

Trinity, the deity of Christ, and the atonement. American Unitarianism, a Protestant Ishmael with its hand against every creedal neighbor, was a rebellious child of New England's Calvinistic theology.

Such a statement, however, while true enough within the geography and historical period under discussion, ignores both the spirit of the period in other than religious considerations, and the ancient lineage of liberal theology throughout Christendom. "Liberalism in America was a humanitarian, and not a theological movement. Boston was liberal before it became Unitarian, and its Unitarianism was primarily ethical and social."[1] For though the Unitarian controversy in America is specifically dated at 1815, Emlyn's *Humble Inquiry into the Scripture Account of Jesus Christ* was circulated in New England nearly sixty years earlier, and Unitarianism itself goes back to England, where Henry VIII had some Baptists burned in 1535 for denying the doctrine of the Trinity; while the ultimate roots of Unitarianism, whatever differences developed in the doctrinal flower, are in the Arian heresy, and that means the fourth century.

In the history of liberal religious thinking, American Unitarianism holds a large place, but here it is enough to recognize the movement and to illustrate its nature by such a survey of the life and character of its representative figure as falls

[1] Haroutunian: *Piety Versus Moralism,* p. 179.

within the scope of the present volume. The representative figure is that of William Ellery Channing, although Theodore Parker forced the Unitarians to express their fundamental beliefs in more precise language, while his own utterances led the orthodox to further definitions of their theology. Channing was born in Newport, Rhode Island, on April 7, 1780, ten years after Whitefield died in Newburyport, and while the American Revolution was stumbling along toward independence and the Republic. His biographer, John White Chadwick, unintentionally records the phenomenal results of Whitefield's ministry as he shows us his hero girding at the religious "enthusiasm" of the Methodists, which Channing regarded as the result of Whitefield's preaching and the religious emotionalism of which it was the expression. It would probably have disturbed Channing to realize how much similarity there was between Whitefield and himself in the experiences which shaped their lives. He was a Harvard product, and seems never to have forgotten it, having graduated from the simple, religiously patterned, eighteenth-century Harvard, in 1798; as Whitefield, though Channing might very easily not have remembered, had received the degree from Oxford, sixty years before. During the two years following his graduation, Channing, a tutor in a Virginia family, had ruined his health by foolish asceticism, as Whitefield had almost done for himself during his Holy Club days at Oxford. But there was, nevertheless, this difference among others, that while Whitefield by sensible conduct completely recovered health robust enough to carry him through thirty-four years of vigorous activity and continuous hardship, Channing by unending precautions maintained intact his physical disabilities, and not only availed himself completely of the comfort which a wealthy marriage afforded him but, as even his most worshipful biographer intimates, resented illness in those around him as an invasion of his own particular domain. Four years after his graduation from Harvard he entered on the study of theology in Cambridge, and a year later, June, 1803, was ordained and installed as minister of the Federal Street Church, Boston. This was, at the time, an orthodox Congregational church, and Channing, to all intents and purposes, was an orthodox clergyman, though suspicions of some of the doctrines of Calvinism had found lodging in his mind. More than suspicions had begun in his boyhood on a day when he had gone with his father to hear a famous preacher of the time, and had been overwhelmed by a sermon rich in Calvinism's most confident and specific description of the hopeless depravity of fallen men and the eternal punishments to be visited upon them by an awful God. The boy was thoroughly convinced that it was all true, and found his opinion confirmed when, after the service, his father remarked to an acquaintance that it was "sound doctrine, sir." On the way home he kept silent because of the terror of what he had heard, and supposed his father was similarly subdued; but his father soon began to whistle and, at home, said nothing whatever about the sermon, but made himself comfortable with slippers and newspaper, as if nothing had happened. Then the boy became sure that his father did not believe that what the preacher had said was true, and that other people did not believe it, and so concluded for himself that it was not true. The grip of Calvinism, of course, was not to be escaped in a single observation of childhood; and during his growing and student years that grip lay constantly upon his mind as upon the thought and faith of his time. There was the influence also of Dr. Samuel Hopkins, the Newport minister, whose parsonage was so near Channing's home that the young man could see the light in the parsonage study as the Doctor worked there early in winter mornings. What few Victorians are left who have not forgotten Harriet Beecher Stowe's *The Minister's Wooing,* will recall her suggestive though not wholly accurate portrayal of Hopkins and his life; but he is perhaps better known for his often quoted declaration, to which reference will be made more than once in these chapters, that men should be willing to be damned for the glory of God. He was born in 1721 and, though seventeen years younger than Jonathan Edwards, was intimately acquainted with him. Channing disclaims having been strongly influenced by him, saying that while Hopkins was perhaps the first preacher he heard, he heard him with no profit, Hopkins's manner making it impossible for a child to be interested. But Hopkins's personal influence upon Channing as a young preacher was inescapable, and Channing in 1836 acknowledged it, although he seems early to have rejected the doctrine of predestination and held, as always, to that of the freedom of the will.

I

The phrase "religiously patterned" as applied to the Harvard which Channing knew is not to be read as a description of undergraduate experience. Harvard participated fully in the social and religious deterioration of the colleges of the period. John White Chadwick quotes from a volume descriptive of life there in Channing's time, "At least one fourth of every class became sots." "College was sometimes suspended for several days, the entire Faculty being employed on the inquest into some recent escapade or outrage."[2] This was before later moralists had discovered that national Prohibition was the most fruitful cause of intemperance and that the one sure way to keep young men and women from drinking to excess was to make liquor run like water through all the fields of social life. Channing's testimony was no better. "College," he said, "was never in a worse state than when I entered it. . . . The tone of books and conversation was presumptuous and daring. . . . The state of morals among the students was anything but good."[3] Just before he entered upon

[2] Chadwick: *William Ellery Channing,* p. 59.
[3] *Ibid.,* p. 35f.

the work of the ministry, Channing joined the First Church in Cambridge, of which the father of Oliver Wendell Holmes was the minister. Doctor Holmes, like the majority of the preachers in the vicinity of Boston, was what was called a Moderate Calvinist. His influence, though unrecognized, probably had some effect on Channing's mind for it was about this time that Channing wrote several articles of belief, in which he may be presumed to have expressed himself. They were for the most part Calvinistic and not without evidence, in spite of Channing's disavowel, that Hopkins had put his mark on the young man; but he was even then close to Arianism in his inclination to believe that Jesus was a being of a single kind, "neither God nor man, nor God and man," but a pre-existent Creator just less than God in eternal and infinite qualities.

The division in the churches between the more conservative Calvinists and the liberals was becoming increasingly acute, and for a time Channing seemed about to take the conservative road, "for," as he himself explained it, "ill health and depression gave me a dark view of things." He adds that it was the doctrine of the Trinity which kept him back, but as his biographer points out, when he actually broke with Congregationalism and went into the organized Unitarian sect, the doctrine of the Trinity was the least of his reasons; and the same biographer kindles an unintentional glow of humor over the subject by writing that Channing's theology was steadily becoming less

Calvinistic "under the influence of improving health and an environment of domestic cheerfulness."[4]

The Federal Street Church, in the ministry of which Channing was installed June 1, 1803, had a place in the sun. The building, fifty-nine years old when Channing was installed, was "small, and phenomenally plain, bare, and ugly even for its time and place."[5] The society had been organized in 1729 by Scotch-Irish Presbyterians who, before the building had been erected, worshiped in a barn. Eleven years after the phenomenally plain structure had been built, it was the seat of the state convention which ratified the federal Constitution, an event that gave the name to the street. The name not only recalls the making of the federal republic; it suggests the sharpness of the political distinctions of the time. Boston's population was twenty-five thousand and there were few strangers in society, yet politics separated social groups as the sheep from the goats. Jeffersonian democrats were called Jacobins, and a lady of the period is quoted as saying that she would have expected to see a cow in a drawing room as soon as a Jacobin. Much later, in 1844, George Bancroft, the historian, had an illuminating experience. He had already begun the publication of his great history. Within a year he was to enter President Polk's cabinet and establish the Naval Academy at Annapolis, and his career was even-

---

[4] Chadwick: *William Ellery Channing,* p. 88.
[5] *Ibid.,* p. 65.

tually to take him as Minister to Great Britain from 1846 to 1849, and to Berlin from 1867 to 1874. He had just made what was called a brilliant candidacy for the governorship of Massachusetts, on the Democratic ticket. As Senator Hoar told the story, Bancroft met on the street a lady of the socially elite and the Whig party and said, "I did not find you at home when I called."

"No," was her reply, "and you never will."

Channing remained a minister of the Federal Street Church from his installation in 1803 until his death in 1842, though in his later years his ill health, his domestic security, his political differences with his congregation, and his engagements elsewhere, resulted in a very few appearances in his own pulpit. Yet while his writings preserve his fame, with few exceptions his books are reprints of sermons and addresses, and it is Channing the preacher who as author has his place in the history of American religious thought.

It is as the preacher that he is remembered, as he was noted in his own time; and there can be few greater contrasts than that between his social influence and his physical qualities and appearance. Short, slight, emaciated, pale, he seemed always on the verge of collapse. The effect was heightened by his constant and excessive care of himself. He was always "bundled up," appearing sometimes in a large red shawl, while with the shawl or its equivalent removed, in the pulpit he was seen to have a heavy belted silk gown under his surplice. Driving in his open country he sometimes wore a green veil to keep the dust from his throat. A parishioner has told of Channing's staying indoors, a depressed invalid for two weeks, because a weather vane pointed northeast, not discovering, until the fact was pointed out to him, that the vane was stuck fast and the wind was from the south and warm. Preaching, as he did, with immense and magnetic vitality, to be distinguished, however, from physical exertion, after each service he was for hours, sometimes for days, in a state of physical and nervous prostration.

When he preached, however, the congregation knew that for the time, his was a master's mind and a prophet's passion. Preaching was for him what it should be for every preacher—"the great action of his life." In the pulpit he maintained the illusion of being very much larger physically than actually he was. His voice was unusually rich, discriminating, and effectual. He read hymns and Scriptures so impressively that congregations listened not as a matter of form but in hushed expectancy. The strength of his preaching, according to the biographer, lay in his conviction of the importance of the message to men's lives. But, on the other hand, when he had apprehended the truth, "he gave it to men. Whether they could accept it or not, he considered that he had done his duty in announcing his discovery." His message was important. Beginning his ministry as a Calvinist, he gave to the liberal protesting groups the most eloquent statement of their faith which, slowly, had become his own. The representative character of his utterances may be understood from the fact that in 1848, six years after Channing's death, a single traveling book agent sold nearly five thousand copies of his writings at two dollars and fifty cents each, and by 1854, twelve years after his death, more than one hundred thousand copies had been sold. Today, but a few years less than a century after his death, Channing's works are still the official literature of American Unitarianism.

II

The history of American Unitarianism and the Unitarian Church constitutes almost a library in itself; in it William Ellery Channing occupied indisputably first place, although he did not initiate any movement, and for a considerable period left his colleagues in doubt as to whether he would go with the liberals or remain among the orthodox.

The controversy of 1815 was begun by the publication of Thomas Belsham's pamphlet *American Unitarianism; or a Brief History of the Progress and Present State of the Unitarian Churches in America,* in which the implications were quite plain that Calvinism's God permitted evil and instead of being a God of love was a God of injustice. The pamphlet argued to the contrary that the blessings which America had enjoyed were evidence that God was favorable and concerned with human happiness; that He forgave sin and, therefore, was a God of love, and rewarded virtue with success, being consequently a God of justice. Into his own work Belsham introduces the creed of Theophilus Lindsey, who instituted the first Unitarian Church in London, with its declaration for "one single person who is God," its description of Jesus as a "man of the Jewish nation, the servant of this God, highly honored and distinguished by Him," and the belief in the Holy Spirit as "only the extraordinary power or gift of God." The controversy which followed was widespread and sharp, with the Unitarians, until Parker's influence became felt, apparently believing that the vagueness of their own definitions permitted them to claim agreement with essential evangelical orthodoxy. Channing attempted to reconcile the two parties, declaring himself unwilling to introduce into his pulpit the controversy over the Trinity which, he said, had no bearing upon life. He said that he had always "cherished the most exalted views of Jesus Christ, which are consistent with the Supremacy of the Father," and announced his disagreement with Belsham "in perhaps every sentiment which is peculiar to him on this subject." But there was no reconciliation; and in the face of the criticism of the orthodox, Channing first developed the martyr pose and then put himself at the head of the liberal group.

In 1819 he preached the sermon at the ordination of Jared Sparks, in Baltimore, and Sparks, with all his own distinguished career in history and in the presidency of Harvard, was said to be more famous because of Channing's sermon at his ordination than by reason of anything else. In it appears Channing's famous statement of the character of God.

> To give our views of God in one word, we believe in His parental character. We ascribe to Him not only the name, but the dispositions and principles of a father. We believe that He has a father's concern for His creatures, a father's desire for their improvement, a father's equity in proportioning His demands to their powers, a father's joy in their progress, a father's readiness to receive the penitent, and a father's justice for the incorrigible. We look upon this world as a place of education, in which He is training men by prosperity and adversity, by aids and obstructions, by conflicts of reason and passion, by motives to duty and temptations to sin, by a various discipline suited to free and moral beings, for union with Himself, and for a sublime and ever-growing virtue in heaven.

This famous "Baltimore Sermon" was Channing's most important contribution to the development and separation of the Unitarian Church into a denomination. In this sermon Channing struck the ethical note which became increasingly predominant in all his utterances and furnished the ground upon which thereafter he more and more diverged from orthodoxy. His biographer, remarking on the critical importance of this sermon, frankly calls attention to the paradox that Channing, who boasted of his hatred of sectarianism, was more influential than any other man in the creating of another sect. But Channing's progress, theologically and socially, was always by advance and recession, so that before he ever came to an unqualified position, he was generally considered to be now on one side and now on the other. The eulogistic John White Chadwick explains it with the least reflection on Channing's forthrightness by saying that he had the Hamlet disposition of holding back from action in the hope of reaching its ideal form. But his contemporaries can be forgiven if at times they did not so much consider him a Hamlet as an opportunist. Hazlitt's fierce criticism was doubtless out of proportion but there was truth enough in it to give the exaggeration currency. Doctor Channing, Hazlitt wrote, "keeps an eye on both worlds; kisses hands to the reading public all around; and does his best to stand in with different sects and parties. He is always in advance of the line, in an animated and imposing attitude, but never far from succor."

What beliefs were gathered into his own body of conviction? Channing's views in some respects were quite evangelical and orthodox; but he began with revolt against Calvinism at the point of its denial of human freedom. According to what was called Consistent Calvinism, man was by nature incapable of knowing God, let alone loving Him, and only divine grace specifically given could regenerate him so as to make it possible for him to know God. The only virtue God considers is, in the famous phrase, love of universal being, and only a special act of His Divine Spirit enables one to attain to this. Man simply has no part in his salvation and is utterly incapable of bettering his own condition, yet, in the ruthless Calvinistic theology, God held him responsible nevertheless.

With this implacable doctrine which impugns either the intelligence or the moral character of God, went the reasoning which justified arbitrary damnation as a glorification of God.

> How could God's hatred of sin be shown except in a universe where sin is to be found? Therefore sin is in the world. But how, again, can His hatred of it be shown except by His awful and eternal punishment of it? But for sin and hell, therefore, this side of God's nature would be imperfect.[6]

It was against such monstrous doctrines that Channing's liberalism primarily arose, although naturally, as years passed, he more and more left the broad ranges of his original orthodoxy behind him.

It is quite curious, unless one takes very clearly into consideration the viewpoint of the time, that Channing believed and taught that the Bible, from Genesis to Revelation, had the unity of a single volume, and never contradicted or differed from itself in any part. When it appeared otherwise, the contradiction must be removed by sound interpretation. Perhaps no clearer evidence could be presented for the claim that Unitarianism was a movement of dissent which rose from the intuition of lay minds and found expression rather than origination in the pulpits of the clergy. For a liberalism originating in critical judgments would surely have begun by reappraising the processes of revelation and the nature of the Scriptures. The

[6] *Pioneers of Religious Liberty in America,* p. 197.

inherent inconsistency of Channing's statement of his own liberalism adds strength to such a conviction. "I cannot but look on human creeds," he wrote, "with feelings approaching contempt. When I bring them into contrast with the New Testament, into what insignificance do they sink!" But he was also writing: "I am surer that my rational nature is from God than that any book is the expression of His will. This light in my own heart is His primary revelation, and all subsequent ones must accord with it, and are, in fact, intended to blend with it and brighten it." The conclusion of such reasoning is inescapable. Every man his own revelation! Subsequent or other revelations are to blend with and brighten, never, apparently, to discipline or correct a mistaken insight. All creeds are contemptible except one's own!

It is the more singular, then, that Channing held to the supernatural values of Christianity, to the historicity of, and, indeed, the necessity for the New-Testament miracles. He selected nearly all of his texts from the New Testament although very seldom he appealed to its authority. He early took the modern position of plenary not verbal inspiration. He was never dogmatic concerning Jesus other than to affirm that the New Testament did not make any claim of deity for Him, and had nothing to say about His double nature which for so long continued to be fundamental in orthodox Christology. Unitarianism has, at times, followed Arius in maintaining that Jesus is similar in nature but not the same as God and is subordinate to Him. It has worn the garments of Socinianism, believing Jesus to have been a man "miraculously conceived and divinely endowed." But Channing accepted neither statement. "I am more and more inclined to believe," so his son reported him as saying, "in the simple humanity of Jesus."

Very naturally he had to come to terms with the doctrine of atonement. It held so large a place and was written in such terrible characters in orthodox Calvinism that his biographer records his attempt, for a time, to adjust himself to it in some fashion; and, for a time, he tried to believe that there was a mysterious recreative efficacy in the death of Jesus. But he reached the place where he rejected it altogether, writing that the mysterious agency of the cross was "our peril which may become our ruin." Bushnell, who had a good deal in common with Channing, later developed the idea of a suffering God, which Channing considered impossible, declaring that while the idea was implicit in the doctrine of atonement it was the supreme defect of the doctrine itself.

Side by side with his rejection of atonement and the deity of Christ, he believed in the resurrection of Jesus and argued with insight and power for personal immortality. He rejected wholly the orthodox conception of man as separated by sin from God, quoting with eloquence if not in scientific exegesis, "If I make my bed in hell, thou art there." It was not until George A. Gordon applied the precisions of his logical mind to the doctrine of eternal punishment that it really began to crumble within the circle of orthodoxy, but Channing anticipated Gordon, in feeling if not in logic. "Infinite, endless punishment," so he wrote, "would make hell the most interesting spot in the universe. All the sympathies of heaven would be turned toward it." The other side of his argument is still a living witness to spiritual reality:

> There is something far worse than outward punishment. It is sin; it is the state of a soul which has revolted from God, which renounces its Father, and hardens itself against Infinite Love; which, endued with divine powers, enthralls itself to animal lusts; which makes gain its God; . . . which, living under God's eye, dreads man's frown or scorn, and prefers human praise to its own calm consciousness of virtue; which tamely yields to temptation, shrinks with a coward's baseness from the perils of duty, and sacrifices its glory and peace in parting with self-control. No ruin can be compared to this.[7]

III

There seems never to have been a time after he reached the age of thought upon religious subjects when he believed in the Trinity. As his biographer suggests, he arrived at liberal principles before he reached Unitarian doctrines, rejecting the Trinity while still retaining a measure of evangelical Calvinism. This is by no means a difficult paradox, as Professor Paul Elmer More would bear witness. As recently as 1927, Professor

[7] Quoted in Chadwick: *William Ellery Channing*, p. 254.

More, tracing the date and cause of the personification of the Holy Spirit, declared that "The Bible as it stands gave to the Infant Church no trinitarian *dogma,* though it did contain a trinitarian *formula.*" The italics are Professor More's, who, preceding this declaration with the statement that there was no dogma of a Trinity in the primitive Church, added the remark which Phillips Brooks would have disputed, that "this dogma was never in our period anything but an intellectual overgrowth of secondary importance."[8] In the long and bitter Unitarian controversy within the churches, Channing seems seldom to have attacked the doctrine of the Trinity in the pulpit, but he called it "the most unintelligible doctrine about which Christians had ever disputed." Likewise he said little against the doctrines of election and total depravity, though he regarded them as "the most injurious errors which ever darkened the Christian world." But his most eloquent argument for Unitarianism, that of appeal to nature, betrays him into a fatal inconsistency which apparently neither he nor his biographer recognized:

> Nature is no Trinitarian. It gives not a hint, not a glimpse of a tripersonal author. Trinitarianism is a confined system, shut up in a few texts, a few written lines, where many of the wisest minds have failed to discover it. It is not inscribed on the heavens and earth, not borne on every wind, not resounding and

[8] Paul Elmer More: *Christ The Word,* pp. 117, 116.

re-echoing through the universe. The sun and stars say nothing of a God of three persons. They all speak of the One Father whom we adore. To our ears one and the same voice comes from God's word and works, a full and swelling strain, growing clearer, louder, more thrilling as we listen, and with one blessed influence lifting up our souls to the Almighty Father.[9]

The sun and stars, it is true, say nothing of a God of three Persons. But, on the other hand, they say nothing against there being three or thirty Gods involved in their creation and maintenance. It is only as Channing exercises a prejudgment in favor of monotheism which, like a magician, he transfers to nature itself, that he can hear the celestial bodies saying anything about *Our Father*. Perhaps he ought not to be held too strictly to account for what theological opinions he proclaimed; for Unitarianism has always put doctrinal beliefs into the background while trying to give itself to ethical service. But it is worth considering, in this connection, how much larger part in social movements the evangelical bodies have taken. The facts seem to support the contention that unselfish social conduct is difficult to maintain apart from positive theological convictions. Channing's theology may also be considered for another reason to have set loosely on him, for he wrote that it is a good plan "ever and anon to make a clean sweep of that to which we have arrived by logical thought, and take a new view," though he did not

[9] Quoted in Chadwick: *William Ellery Channing,* p. 162.

explain how one was to do it and still remain logical.

Unitarianism, with its practical concern for ethical expression, may naturally be expected to be aggressive in social reform. Channing, with the Hamlet-like vacillations to which reference has been made, had his part in the social reform of the time. From his tutoring days in Virginia he was an enemy of slavery, yet the Missouri Compromise which shook the country in 1820 nowhere appears in his sermons, diary, or correspondence. During a visit to the West Indies in 1830 he began a pamphlet entitled *Slavery,* which when finally published proved to be eloquent and powerful propaganda. But he found Abolitionism unpopular and deferred publication for several years. After the first edition he eliminated the most telling part of the pamphlet, its detailed evidence of slave masters' cruelty and licentiousness, because, as he said, he did not wish to divert the reader's attention from the principles he was arguing. Perhaps no one as much a reformer at heart as Channing more thoroughly illustrates a dictum of Reinhold Niebuhr's which of course no one had phrased in Channing's time. Writing in a fairly recent symposium, Doctor Niebuhr said, "Certainly no just society will ever be built merely by projecting an ethical goal for it."[10] Someone, however, has to set ethical goals before anyone can start intelligent or even madly directed technics

[10] Arthur L. Swift, Jr.: *Religion Today,* p. 154.

in motion toward the achievement of them. In this lay Channing's strength which must not be overlooked in any preoccupation with his weaknesses. The editor of Harriet Martineau's *Autobiography* refers to his vacillation on the greatest social question of the century by saying that Channing

> was touched by Brougham's eloquent denial of the right of property in man, and he adopted the idea as a theme; but he dreaded anyone who claimed, on behalf of the slaves, that their masters should instantly renounce that right of ownership; he was terror-stricken at the idea of calling on the whole American people to take counsel on so difficult and delicate a matter in anti-slavery associations; and, above all, he deprecated the admission of the colored race to our ranks. He had been selected by a set of money-making men as their representative for piety, as Edward Everett was their representative gentleman and scholar, Judge Story their representative jurist and companion in social life, and Daniel Webster their representative statesman and advocate looking after their interests in Congress.

Channing's loyalty to principles rather than specifications is seen in his remark that to him the slaveholder was little more than abstraction. Yet with his undoubted earnestness for emancipation, his interest in John Brown, and his noble protest after Lovejoy's assassination, he did not accept an invitation to meet William Lloyd Garrison. Liberalism, in Channing, was alert in every social and political occasion. His eighty-page open letter to Henry Clay on "The Annexation of

Texas" was widely circulated, and Mrs. Chapman, whose sharp criticism of him was just quoted above, gave her opinion that it had delayed the annexation for years.

No one with Channing's respect for men as men, and his singularly scrupulous concern for ethical righteousness, could fail to be active in movements against war and intemperance, and on behalf of social justice, education, and peace. The peace society of Massachusetts was begun in his own home. He was interested in experiments like Brook Farm and others of its kind. A kindlier light falls on his small, invalid figure and his habit of detachment, as he is seen writing the first subscription to Father Taylor's new Seamen's Bethel. His Federal Street Church was also the first in which Father Taylor presented the claims of his work and received a collection; while Channing again and again went to the Bethel to hear the seamen's evangelist preach. On his part Father Taylor did not fail of appreciating Channing. "He has splendid talents," Father Taylor once said, "what a pity he has not been educated!"

Channing died, after long, slow ebbing of his precarious strength, on October 2, 1842. It was Sunday, and he had a friend read to him from the Sermon on the Mount. After the Lord's Prayer, his voice failed with his last words, "I have received many messages from the Spirit."

They turned him in his bed, that he might look upon the eastern hills, on which, and on the sky above them, the reflected sunset light was warm and beautiful. Through the parted curtains and a clambering vine, it stole in upon his face. None knew just when he passed, but he died looking eastward, as if expectant of another dawn.[11]

New-England Calvinism was not yet frightened for its strongholds, but might well have been, for the liberal winds were rising. Unitarianism was not the final answer to the need of perplexed souls. But its more tender and reasonable views of God, its recapture of the New Testament ideal of the kingdom of God on earth, rather than in the spectacularism of a remorseless hell and a feudal heaven; its vision of Christ no longer removed from the highways of our common life by the mysterious and forensic separations of a harsh theology, were sapping at Calvinism's forbidding doctrines like sea waves crumbling unobserved at castle walls. It was not a preacher, even Channing, or many preachers together whose pulpits wrought its eventual doom. It was the spreading liberalism in logical minds whose spokesmen and guides the liberal preachers were. But preachers were the spokesmen; they gave form and direction to what otherwise might have remained inarticulate intuitions and feelings. They organized the diffused convictions into an ordered and recognized body of belief. They created the literature not only of a sect but of a movement for intellectual freedom, and the name of names among them is William Ellery Channing.

[11] Chadwick: *William Ellery Channing,* p. 42.

References

Chadwick, John W., *Theodore Parker.*

Chadwick, John W., *William Ellery Channing.*

Channing, William H., *Life of William Ellery Channing.*

Cooke, G. W., *Unitarianism in America.*

Eliot, Charles W., *Four American Leaders.*

Frothingham, O. B., *Theodore Parker.*

Frothingham, O. B., *Transcendentalism in New England.*

Mathews, Thomas S., *Channing—A Study.*

Parrington, V. L., *Main Currents in American Thought,* Vol. II.

Perry, Bliss, *The Spirit of American Literature.*

Spiller, R. E., "A Case for W. E. Channing," in *New England Quarterly,* Vol. III.

VI

HORACE BUSHNELL: THE BELOVED HERETIC

VI

HORACE BUSHNELL: THE BELOVED HERETIC

Horace Bushnell was born on April 14, 1802, in a Connecticut village from which his parents very soon afterward removed, some fourteen miles, to a community where his father engaged in farming, and wool carding and cloth dressing by machinery. The boy Bushnell grew up at home with both industries, working in each from the time he was old enough until he became of age. Both occupations and their environments left their marks upon him in his unusual responsiveness to nature and his persistent interest in engineering and mechanics.

His father had been reared under the religious influence of a devout Unitarian mother; the boy's own mother was a consistent member of the Protestant Episcopal Church; and inasmuch as both of his parents were concerned for religion rather than for distinctive and exclusive theologies, it was as easy as it was natural for them to unite with the Congregational Church in the home to which they went soon after the boy's birth. Neither of them participated in the rigid Calvinism of the Church of their adoption, though Mrs. Bushnell sometimes sought to soften her husband's more vehement protests against what he called the tough predestination and over-depravity of the preaching. Bushnell himself, in after years, claimed to take satisfaction in the fact that, as he put it, he had been episcopally regenerated.

His thoughtful life began rather early. His mother taught him music and planned his education, and was particularly responsible for his securing it. He was but seventeen years old and was still working at a wool-carding machine when he wrote a paper in which he attempted—of all intellectual occupations for a seventeen-year-old boy!—to make Calvinism consistent and, as Theodore Munger wrote, "correct Saint Paul's willingness to be accursed for the sake of his brethren." At nineteen he joined the church and when he was twenty-one, having gone through the local academy, he set out for Yale, from which he graduated in 1827. He taught school, as most college graduates of his time did, though for not longer than several months, and there are few of us today who do not sympathize with his remark that he would rather lay a stone wall any time. For ten months he was employed in writing for the New York *Journal of Commerce,* he studied in the New Haven Law School for half a year, and still groping for a definite career, accepted an appointment as tutor in Yale College. About this same time he discovered that his personal religion had left him. While he had been busy here and there it had escaped.

During the winter of 1831 a revival of religion came upon the college, as was more customary then than now, and in the fine old phraseology of our religious past, he came under conviction. It was not, however, a conviction of sin as much as it was a conviction of responsibility. His responsibility for the students under his care weighed provocatively upon him; and he was converted, as his biographer has written, "to duty rather than faith, but he made the discovery that faith could wait, but duty could not."[1]

The theology of the day failed to satisfy him, but duty became the voice of God and he felt himself unmistakably called to the Christian ministry. Entering New Haven Theological School in 1831, two years later he was installed as minister of the North Church, Hartford. His long and fruitful ministry in that church to which he gave distinction does not fall within the survey of his personal character and the contribution he made to American religious life and thought, but it is of interest to recall that at the time of his installation into its pulpit the church, with its parish as well, was sharply divided into Old and New Theological parties. It was his own personal experience that was in his mind when, in an anniversary sermon twenty years later, he described the "young pastor, who is to be thus daintily inserted between an acid and an alkali; having it for his task both to keep them apart and to save himself from being bitten of one or devoured by the other."

The time in which Bushnell began his ministry in Hartford has been called the critical period in the life of the churches, although the remark need

[1]Munger: *Horace Bushnell,* p. 27.

not be taken too seriously, as every time and every generation have been called critical for the churches. "That Bush," as Samuel Rutherford wrote in 1637, "has been burning these five thousand years, and no man yet saw the ashes of that fire." Theodore Munger characterized the years of Bushnell's early ministry and the situation prevailing in religious thought by saying that the

> New-England Theology had worn itself out by the friction of its own conflicting elements. Edwards was no longer a name to conjure with. The main current of his influence had gone to feed an intellectual idealism, and his specific theology had been "improved" under so many different forms that it could hardly be recognized. The general criticism to be made as a whole, is that Edwards's avowed purpose was the overthrow of an alleged heresy. He incurred the weakness of a negative method. He assumed that if Arminianism were overthrown, Calvinism would hold the ground. The mistake was a fatal one, because it substituted controversy for investigation.[2]

Correct as Doctor Munger's analysis was, his remark that the New-England Theology had worn itself out overstates the truth except as its reference is limited to the realm of dialectic. In the regions of practical influence as registered in the qualifications required in candidates for Congregational pulpits and theological chairs, it was still dominant; and it still occupied first place in the minds of the majority of lay members however it may have failed to satisfy them. Munger was writ-

[2] Munger: *Horace Bushnell,* pp. 35, 36.

ing in 1899 and was perhaps too close to events to perceive that the actual collapse of the New-England theology was not to be indubitably recorded until an October night in 1884.

Something of the yeasty and disintegrating energies at work within the body of New-England Calvinism can be glimpsed in a hurried survey of a few men who, in their time, were considered of more than ordinary importance. Not all the theologians of New England can be discussed, or need be named for the purpose, unless a thoroughness of detail is required such as can be found in Herbert Wallace Schneider's *The Puritan Mind.* For a satisfactory appreciation of the world into which Bushnell entered, the world which he was greatly to change, six men will serve: Joseph Bellamy, Samuel Hopkins, Nathanael Emmons, Jonathan Edwards, Jr.—the Younger Edwards, as he is called—Timothy Dwight, Nathaniel W. Taylor; these will illustrate the theological atmosphere and the debates of the period. They were unanimous in their conviction that Arminianism was their common antagonist and objective and each bravely set out to correct and "improve" the theology of Jonathan Edwards, from whom theologically they all derived.

Professor Whitehead has affirmed within recent years that it is upon the reality of evil that all simplifications of religious dogma are wrecked; which was as true a hundred years ago as it is today. The very crux and citadel at which theology was tested in the days upon which Bushnell entered was its treatment of the fact of sin; and the New-England theologians did not all ultimately justify their courage. Bellamy, with Calvinism behind, and the evil in life and experience before him, said that this world is holier and happier as it is than it would have been if there had been no evil at all. He argued for the claim which is now quite familiar that sin is necessary for the achievement of the highest good—a contention which can probably be defended as a universal principle but which he, as Doctor Munger comments, mistakenly limited to theology. Hopkins accepted Jonathan Edwards's definition of virtue as a love of being in general, and from it argued to the establishment of disinterested benevolence. This might seem at first to be of only academic import, and the logic by which Hopkins reached his conclusion is "as faultless as it is unconvincing." But when it was practically applied to its farthest absolutely logical result, it is issued in the famous Calvinist duty of being willing to be damned for the glory of God. Emmons, holding steadfastly to belief in God as Universal Cause, went the full distance and considered God as the cause of sin itself; but he introduced a new and startling element into his thinking by claiming that the soul is a series of exercises. That, of course, brought him quite unintentionally, but no less certainly, straight into pantheism. The Younger Edwards "improved" his father's famous and monumental dealing with the Will, and while holding firmly to the orthodox Calvinism of divine sovereignty, he opened the way for the Grotian theory of atonement by Substitution. President Timothy Dwight accused all of these theologians with being pantheists and broke clearly away from original Calvinism by arguing for the freedom of the Will as stubbornly as any Arminian. He rejected the idea that righteousness can be imputed to men and urged that means to salvation are necessary and must be cultivated, a procedure which, in the older days of pure and triumphant Calvinism, had been considered not only useless but positively wicked. Nathaniel W. Taylor argued that sin is not necessary in the human order, but is only incidental; although he once declared to one of the Beechers that the smallest and most incidental sin deserved eternal punishment. He put himself also side by side with President Dwight by asserting without equivocation that the human Will had the power of self-determination.

All of these theologians, as Doctor Munger says, agreed and disagreed with Edwards and with each other, but all were fairly good Calvinists. Yet while they said that their disagreements with Jonathan Edwards were "improvements," and apparently did not so much as suspect that they were opening the door to Arminianism, when Taylor made his assertions of sin as incidental and the Will as self-determining, Calvinist though he claimed to be, Arminianism had come boldly in at the very door and was at home in the house of Calvinism itself.

What strikes a modern reader, of course, is the

fact that these themes on which the New-England theologians were most eloquent and sure are the subjects on which Christ said nothing at all. And these are the minds and the diverse interests of what has been called the noblest period in the history of New-England theology. There was no promise of unanimity in such theological enterprises, and when in 1828 Taylor's preaching gave publicity to his views, the period became one of very definite theological disunity. Orthodoxy was divided; churches were ranged in opposing and by no means inarticulate camps; and theological schools were established, much after the fashion which we have more recently seen in Philadelphia, in order specifically to foster and defend the theology of the past from Taylor's Arminian modernism. This was the period into which, in 1831, Bushnell entered from a home where, amid the orthodoxy of the Church his parents had joined from two quite different communions, there was no Calvinistic atmosphere.

It is not necessary to follow laboriously Bushnell's career from the beginning of his ministry. His characteristic attitudes and patterns of thought as well as the direction of his intellectual and spiritual development can be observed in some isolated and somewhat familiar utterances. The first of his sermons to be published appeared in 1833, provoked by the mobbing of William Lloyd Garrison in the streets of Boston. The subject of the sermon was one which probably every preacher has used at some time in his ministry and is one which has a curiously familiar sound at the present time. It was "The Crisis in the Church." The sermon is, naturally, of no great interest now, but it attracted considerable attention at the time of its delivery by reason of the remark in it that Protestantism in religion produces republicanism in government; and because, also, of its outspoken declaration that the principal dangers to the country were "slavery, infidelity, Romanism, and the current of our political tendencies." One is immediately reminded of the "Rum, Romanism, and Rebellion" speech of Doctor Burchard which wrecked Blaine's election to the Presidency in 1884. During that same year of 1833 Bushnell published another sermon on "Duty Not Measured by Our Ability," in which he supported the principle "that men are often, and properly, put under obligation to do that for which they have, in themselves, no present ability." Both the Old-School and the New-School Calvinists discussed at length natural ability, and talked much about what they called moral ability and gracious ability, but, as Bushnell said, they "raised a false issue which can never be settled." These are slight enough incidents, but they serve to illustrate the significant intellectual process going on in the young preacher's mind to which twenty years after his ordination he referred when he said that he had then been "passing into a vein of comprehensiveness, questioning whether all parties were not, in reality, for one side or article of the truth."

This quality of comprehensiveness is still more

clearly recognized in his utterances during a controversy of some moment in 1844, a controversy which has been described as made up of practical politics and theological subtleties of a Jesuitical hue. The question propounded at first was whether it is right to vote for either a duelist or an oppressor of the poor for the Presidency. A characteristic answer was given by Hopkins that "if two devils were candidates for office and one of them was certain to be elected, it would be a man's duty to vote for the lesser devil; otherwise he would be responsible for the evil committed by the greater devil." Bushnell, in an article published in a periodical in December, 1844, took the question entirely out of the region of expediency and put it into the sphere of morality by arguing that to vote for bad men on such a principle as Hopkins defended would, as Bushnell's biographer commented later, organize immorality into the life of the nation and so fail of the greater good. "The point he made," so the biographer, Doctor Munger, has explained, "underlay the antislavery movement, the resistance to the fugitive slave law, the outcry of the North against Webster's seventh-of-March speech, and entered into the thought that issued in the Free Soil Party."[3] N. W. Taylor's contribution to the controversy was to maintain that consequences create duty, which was, in fact, the principle upon which political action in the country had been and continued to

[3] Munger: *Horace Bushnell*, p. 45.

be conducted for a good many years. Bushnell's reply to that was that the only consequences worth having are products of righteousness; and, as Doctor Munger again points out, it was that sort of principle which carried the North through the Civil War and ultimately ended slavery in America.

In 1849 Bushnell's volume, *God in Christ,* appeared, and the storm which had been darkening on the horizons around him broke in full force. The germ of the volume was in a sermon which he had preached, though curiously enough in neither the sermon nor the book did he deny any of the cardinal doctrines of the New-England faith. What he did was to marshall them in quite new and wholly unaccustomed formulas in such aggressive and rather inescapable fashion that the entire armament of the New-England Theology was aroused. Three articles, written at Yale, were published in *The Biblical Repository and Princeton Review.* In Boston *The Christian Observatory* printed an article of sixty hostile pages. The Bangor Theological Seminary put out its review and criticism of the book in a volume of a hundred and twenty-five pages. And the Theological Seminary at East Windsor, while it did not issue a formal review of Bushnell's offending volume, carried on a prolonged guerilla warfare against it and against Bushnell, in *The Religious Herald.*

If the sober-minded readers of those solemn publications had any sense of humor, there must have been a good deal of godly merriment in New England during that year of 1849. For during the controversy and in their respective publications, the theological seminaries of New Haven, Bangor, and Princeton flatly contradicted one another on the atonement; while Doctor Goodrich of Yale argued for a theory of the Person of Christ which Doctor Hodge of Princeton declared had never been heard of. Naturally enough, an attempt was made through the proper channels to bring Bushnell to trial for heresy; and, naturally enough also, the attempt failed, and for several reasons. It was difficult then, as it is difficult now, to secure a heresy trial in the Congregational system; while, in addition, a good many intelligent men who read the book and honestly disagreed with its author, did not believe that his opinions were heretical. Another very efficient cause for the inability to secure Bushnell's trial for heresy was the fact that the New Haven Seminary which led in the attack on him and his lack of orthodoxy had been so often charged with heresy itself, that its accusation of anyone else impressed its contemporaries as rather less than convincing; particularly as, generally speaking, about half the clergy of Connecticut were called heretics by the other half.

Effective as these several preventives were in making a heresy trial impossible, it is not at all certain that they were the deepest and most powerful of the restraints. Something might be said for the imponderable force of a veracious and revealing experience such as that out of which Bushnell's book had come. His child had died in 1843, the effect being a personal sorrow of peculiar tenacity, of which we are reminded later when, in a discussion of the reality of heaven, he asked, "Have I not a harper there?" During the years immediately following this bereavement he read Fénelon and a good deal of the literature of mysticism, and then, very early one February morning in 1838, as Mrs. Bushnell told the incident in her story of his life, she awoke to find him radiant with a new discovery and was told that the light for which they had both been waiting so long had come to him. She asked him, "What have you seen," and his reply, now part of the imperishable language of religion, was "The gospel." It was out of that experience that he preached his sermon on "Christ the Form of the Soul," and followed the sermon a year later with the volume, *God in Christ.* It would have been a strange dislocation of spiritual values if the product of such an experience, which Bushnell himself regarded as his personal discovery of Christ and of God as represented in Him, could have been arraigned as heresy.

A dozen years after the book was published, and all thought of trying its author had long since been dead, a young preacher dissatisfied with the prevailing theology and wondering whether, after all, there were a gospel to preach, came upon the volume, and was at once and forever, as he said, delivered from the bondage of an immoral theology and from his own doubt, by being "made to see that the Judge of the earth would do right." "That," he said, "was the foundation of Bushnell's faith; his heresy was the unfaltering belief that God is just. What he denied was simply those assertions and implications of the old theology which attribute to God injustice."[4]

No chapter on Bushnell would be complete without reference to the words with which he closed his life on earth. It was on February 17, 1876, that he died, having just said to those who watched his translation, "Well, now, we are all going home together; and I say, the Lord be with you—and in grace—and peace—and love—and that is the way I have come along home." So, in simplicity and tenderness and faith he died as, underneath the storm that beat over him, lived the thinker who has been called, second to Theodore Parker, the most original and influential theologian in New England in the last half of the nineteenth century. How far, and to what regions different from those in which he himself lived, his influence reached is seen in Washington Gladden's testimony:

> I could not have remained in the ministry an honest man if it had not been for him. The time came, long before I saw him, when the legal or forensic theories of the atonement were not true for me; if I had not found his "God in Christ" and "Christ in Theology" I must have stopped preaching. Doctor Bushnell gave me a moral theology, and helped me to believe in the justice of God. If I have had any gospel to preach during the last thirty-five years, it is because he led me into the light and joy of it.[5]

[4] Washington Gladden: *Recollections*, p. 119.
[5] Munger: *Horace Bushnell*, p. 375.

It sounds very much like a paradox to say, after such a testimony from such a man as Doctor Gladden, that Bushnell was not a great theologian, but the fact lies in just that word. He had not the systematic mind of the scientific theologian. He was not careful for consistency. Paraphrasing one of his own striking sentences it is to be said of him that when he had undertaken to find the truth, he was never willing to be excused from further obligations because the truth seemed to be outgrowing his published expositions. Professor John Wright Buckham appraised Bushnell's intellectual method accurately and fairly by saying that he spoke his first thoughts without waiting for his second, much less for his third; and it is third thoughts which count for most in any area of truth. Bushnell himself said the same thing only he said it in the mood and language of poetry, which was so much more characteristic of him than the precisions of theology. "Finding the air full of wings about me, buoyant and free, I let them come under and lift."

That is not the language of a theologian but it reflects the major service which Bushnell wrought, which was greater perhaps than that accomplished by any theologian of his time or the generations immediately before him. He brought theology back to Christ. The New-England theology into which Bushnell was inducted was thoroughly Calvinistic, having, it is true, a place for Christ; but it was wholly a theological Christ precisely fitted into a rigorously articulated "Plan of Redemption" which was convincing in proportion to the distance the gospel was left behind. Bushnell refused instinctively to move away from the gospel.

That is not to say that his Christology is in all points satisfactory. He was not theologian enough to make it so. His inconsistency and unsystematic process of thought vitiated his metaphysics, of which it might be said that he was quite unconscious. He read the Gospels with little if any critical purpose or concern and was apparently a stranger to any distinctions such as are suggested by the now familiar phraseology of the Jesus of History and the Christ of Faith. He gives too much and too emphatic place to the virgin birth; and his inconsistency reveals itself in the fact that, having declared that man is himself a supernatural being, that the divine and human are essentially unity, he throws away the position by discriminating sharply between them and placing Jesus wholly on the divine side.

But all this being true, his service to theology and to personal religion has been inestimable because of the reality of Christ which he restored, not only writing of it but by living it amid the bitterness and storm which broke around him because of the utterances by which he did his share in saving a generation from the hopelessness and harshness and unreasonableness of the New-England theology.

That restoration of Christ to the center of theology was the result of what had been going on in his life which he described on that early morning when he said he had seen the gospel. It would take far wiser mind and deeper insight than this writer possesses, far wiser and deeper than have been revealed by any of his biographers, to trace and date the various stages of his spiritual development which culminated in that vision of the gospel. It is enough for the purposes of this chapter to say that the truth he reached he phrased when he wrote of what he called "A Perceptive Power in Spiritual Life." "It wants a Christed man," he said again, "to know who Christ really is and to show Him forth with a meaning."[6] Theology, that is to say, is the flower of experience; which was a conception so foreign to the New-England religious literature from which Bushnell was in perpetual disagreement as to warrant the belief that it was foreign to the New-England religious life. The New-England theologians can well be described in Carlyle's characterization of John Stuart Mill—as logic-chopping machines; with Bushnell it was the heart that made the theologian, and naturally change, open-mindedness, inconsistency triumphed over dogmatism and system and made his books and sermons homiletical scandals to the theological elite.

He has often been cited as an enemy to Revivals and Revivalism; but as early as 1838 a published paper of his on "The Spiritual Economy of Revivals of Religion," while critical of much that transpired in the revivals of his day, really at-

[6] *Sermons on Living Subjects,* "The Gospel of the Face."

tempted to make clear the much larger range of God's activities and methods and the place of revivals in them as constituting "an ebb and flow measured only by the pulses of the Spirit." It was a paper not out of harmony with the volume on *Christian Nurture,* which appeared eight years later and constituted the first great and undoubtedly the most effective contribution to the rescue of childhood from the New-England theology's treatment of it. Professor Buckham quotes Harriet Beecher Stowe as saying that "With all New England's earnestness and practical efficiency, there is a long withering of the soul's more ethereal portion—a crushing out of the beautiful;" and in no realm was this withering and crushing more deadly than in its conduct of the religion of childhood. It was against this cruel error that Bushnell, two years before the publication of *Christian Nurture,* wrote his article, reprinted in that volume, on "Growth, Not Conquest, the True Method of Christian Progress." In it he wrote an indictment which, familiar and unnecessary as it may seem to be today, was a frontal attack of unprecedented surprise and effectiveness ninety years ago:

> Our very theory of religion is that men are to grow up in evil and be dragged into the Church of God by conquest. The world is to lie in halves and the kingdom of God is to stretch itself side by side with the kingdom of darkness, making sallies into it and taking captive those who are sufficiently hardened and bronzed in guiltiness to be converted. Thus we assume even the absurdity of all our expectations in

regard to the possible advancement of human society and the universal prevalence of Christian virtue. And thus we throw an air of extravagance and unreason over all we do.[7]

Twelve years later he completed the exposition inaugurated in *Christian Nurture,* with his most cataclysmic book on *Nature and the Supernatural,* which destroyed the age-long separation that not only the New-England theology but Christian theology, Catholic and Protestant, from the beginning had maintained between the spiritual and the natural. The inconsistency into which his treatment of Christ took him has been mentioned; but that inconsistency does not vitiate the significance of the attack he made on the historic error, or the tremendous implication of his conclusion that personality is a spiritual reality not wholly under the law of cause and effect because it can set causes in new combinations which otherwise would never so occur and produce results which nature without the action of personality upon it could never of itself produce. That is to say that men are not so much natural and the subjects of supernatural activity and purpose; they are themselves part of the supernatural side of the universe.

Two generations have come and gone since he died, and his books are but little read today. Yet the effect of them and of him has not yet died. *Christian Nurture* and *Nature and the Supernatu-*

---

[7] *Christian Nurture,* p. 25f.

ral are not simply titles of volumes but little used; they have passed into the living structure of present-day religious thinking. They and Bushnell's sermons wrought themselves into the minds and lives of strong men who, through the alembic of their own thought and character, transmitted them to their contemporaries. Brooks, Gladden, Gordon and a host of humbler and unnamed men whose works follow them took their direction from his compass and found illumination at his insights. The body of reasoning into which he cast his discernments may lie moldering among the theological graves, but his spirit goes marching on.

References

Bushnell Centenary, addresses published by the General Association of Connecticut in honor of Bushnell in 1902.

Cheney, Mary Bushnell, *Life and Letters of Horace Bushnell.*

Dole, C. F., "Horace Bushnell and His Work for Theology," in *The New World,* December, 1899.

Munger, T. T., *Horace Bushnell, Preacher and Theologian.*

Munger, T. T., "The Secret of Horace Bushnell," in his *Essays for the Day,* 1904.

Trumbull, H. C., *My Four Religious Teachers.*

VII

PHILLIPS BROOKS: A PROPHETIC GOODNESS

VII

PHILLIPS BROOKS: A PROPHETIC GOODNESS

To mention Phillips Brooks is to remind oneself of the figure in the great pulpit tradition of America whom the adjective "noble" best describes. In physical appearance, in personal manner, in social eminence, in intellectual conduct, in religious influence Phillips Brooks was eminently a noble spirit. From the beginning of his public ministry to the end of his eminent and honored career he gave himself wholly to the enrichment and interpretation of his generation.

Born of a Unitarian mother, his father a Congregationalist, his traceable ancestry went back for nine generations of culture and Puritanism. When he was four years old, his parents merged their ecclesiastical loyalties by uniting with the Episcopal Church, the only organized religious society in the community. To the advantage of his birth, at which the robust intelligence of two Protestant traditions attended, were thus added the disciplines of a communion in which liturgical beauty, a recognition of the rights of history, and an admonishing social pride fostered a self-sustaining dignity of mind.

In his childhood and youth Brooks evidenced no special signs of unusual gifts. He graduated from what has been called the old Harvard of the humanities, which doubtless prepared him to be, as Professor Brastow described him, "the great Christian humanist of his generation"; but the practical value of his training at Cambridge did not at first disclose itself. After graduation he failed as a teacher and, on the advice of one of his Harvard instructors and friends, entered the Protestant Episcopal Seminary at Alexandria, Virginia, where the latent genius of the man continued to be latent. He preached a sermon before the Seminary, in the usual course of homiletical training, on the theme, "The Simplicity of Christ." The comments by his classmates and faculty were not reassuring; the most vivid of them being that in the sermon there was "very little simplicity and no Christ."

During his seminary course he was particularly interested in historic theology, which he followed very carefully in the Church Fathers, showing in this a curious similarity to J. H. Newman, although Brooks's reading did not take him by a hair's breadth in the direction which Newman had traveled fifteen years before. This body of reading remained a positive, if not always recognized influence in his life, one of its consequences undoubtedly being his allegorical preaching. Beyond this interest in Patristic theology his reading ranged perhaps more widely than that of any other student of his day, particularly in the classics and English literature. But all of his reading, regardless of its range, at every period of his career from his Seminary days to his Episcopal office, converged upon his preaching; and when he died in 1893 he was recognized, as he is recognized today, as the greatest American preacher of his generation.

That is rather easily remarked more than forty years later, but his generation was a period of great preachers. It was the generation of Henry Ward Beecher, of Dwight L. Moody, of T. DeWitt Talmage, of Theodore Munger, of Matthew Simpson, to name the outstanding figures of its pulpit. Beecher was far more versatile in the range of his subjects, his interests, and his activities. One heard him, as one reads him now, and repeats Dryden's famous comment on Chaucer: "Here is God's plenty!" Moody was more popularly and emotionally and simply commanding, through his revival meetings; and the more we have had of the hippodrome evangelism of recent years, now receding, the more superior and sane Moody shows himself to have been. Talmage was more dramatic and advertised and widely read; but he was a compiler rather than a thinker, a verbal showman rather than a sober guide of life. Theodore Munger was more intellectual in a dry, white-light sort of fashion, than Brooks; and Simpson, on his great occasions, was more powerful, more stirring, perhaps more overmastering in a way that subdued and exalted the spirit like a beneficent storm. But judged by the depth and permanence of the influence he exercised and the guidance he furnished over a long period of years, unrestricted by class or church or intellectual dividing lines, Phillips

Brooks stood and stands easily at the head of the preachers of his generation and ours.

He was a minister of an exclusive and fairly narrow Communion. His immediate contemporaries in the pulpit were scholars whose names were and still remain of more than continental repute. He preached in a generation during which denominational lines were held hard and fast and theological orthodoxy was very acute and important. Yet he was undenominational and broad in his interests and sympathies; he was not a scholar; he cared little for denominational distinctions and nothing for denominational differences; and without waking a word of responsible criticism, without frightening the most rigid orthodoxy of mind unbiased by other considerations, he preached a Gospel which contravened contemporary orthodoxy and was, himself, the spiritual leader and re-enforcement of preachers and laymen of every Church and creed. He has had no successor.

Before discussing Brooks's contribution to the permanent religious tradition of America it is almost necessary to say a word about Henry Ward Beecher, for Beecher rendered a specific service that will do duty as a frame into which, both in respect of positive content and definite contrast, the portrait of Phillips Brooks will the better fit. It was not the service which remains most prominent in the recollection of the average man who remembers Beecher at all; nor is it always given the eminence it deserves in the sketchy biographies of him. We most easily remember the service which Beecher rendered during the Civil War: his semisensationalism from time to time; as when, for instance, he took a young Negro girl into his pulpit on a Sunday morning and either thrilled or shocked the nation with the plea he made for emancipation. We remember more soberly and gratefully his work during the war when he faced hostile English audiences, stood unfrightened before howling crowds that tried to hiss him down, and by his sheer reasoning and eloquence went farther than any other single influence in keeping the British government from recognizing the Confederacy. Oliver Wendell Holmes said of this mission of Beecher's to England that it constituted "a more remarkable embassy than any envoy who has represented us in Europe since Franklin pleaded the cause of the young republic at the court of Versailles." That great service will always be recorded in our national history; but it was not the largest service that Beecher rendered, and, of course, it had no part in the service he rendered in shaping the course of American religious thought.

He was occupying Plymouth pulpit, in Brooklyn, one of the half-dozen foremost pulpits in America at the time. He was being given probably a wider hearing than that accorded to any other preacher on the continent when the new scientific theory of evolution broke upon American orthodoxy with the effect of an eighteen-inch shell in a convent. The religious leaders of America thought they saw in the theory the final word in sheer atheism, and the ageless controversy between religion and science went into the most acute stage of battle that it has known in modern times. The result threatened to be, indeed, a new wave of atheism, not because of what the preachers and orthodox lay majority feared, but from the unfortunate reaction of thoughtful people to the uncompromising attitude of the clergy in denial. It was a question of evidence founded on facts against interpretations of the Bible born of tradition coming down from a prescientific age. The preachers and religious teachers sought, as too often they have done, to fit facts into their immemorial and splendid but unvindicated tradition or else to deny the facts altogether. The scientific teachers were determined to follow the facts no matter where the facts took them, and on their part too often gave reason for the inference that they hoped the facts would lead them away from religious faith. The younger minds, particularly those coming under the spell of the scientific disciplines of the eighties, followed the scientists, as they have always done. Beecher, braving the condemnation of his reactionary brethren who, of course, were in the majority, took the theory of evolution into his pulpit as he had taken the Negro girl, and made equally eloquent pleas for the emancipation of the mind; showing what is so simple and accepted a thesis now that one is embarrassed at laboring the point, namely, that evolution is a method of creation, not a substitute for it; that it does not contradict essential faith but illumines it; that it need not weaken Christian confidence but may enlarge and re-enforce it. It was Beecher who, more than any other preacher, made the first pathway for the average religious mind of his day from an unscientific to a scientific view of the world, and more than any other man at the time saved the religious situation in a day of misapprehended scientific change.

In that debate Phillips Brooks, open-minded as he was to the new views of truth, took no such prominent and specific part. Just as he served the federal cause during the war, preaching with intense patriotism but with no such dramatic popularity or wide influence as Beecher achieved, so, having a mind more disciplined in scientific knowledge than Beecher's, he was on the side of the new views without being disturbed in his theology nor disturbing that of others. It was not that he did not recognize the issues involved. He knew more theology than Beecher knew, more than his preaching revealed to the listener; but his spiritual life did not feed itself disproportionately upon theology. He had more than a working knowledge of philosophy and its resources for the understanding of life; and he read wisely and constantly in biography, and so had ever fresh insights into the way life works itself out in significant persons. More than either of these restraining and sustaining influences was the fact that his life, like his religion, was a verifiable experience and his preaching was rooted in that experience. Those who knew him recognized that religion was not only the supreme influence which he felt in his personal life, but that for him to tell to others that such was the fact was the most natural thing in the world. So it was that he had as large if not a larger place than Beecher in the great change which during his lifetime came over the thoughts and beliefs of orthodoxy. He was the prophet of a transition period who, though perhaps unconsciously, more than any other man represents and may be said to have led the movement of American Protestantism from the harsh and theological exclusiveness of Puritan New England into the sunnier and more liberal fraternity of modern times.

I

If the essential and pre-eminent impression which Brooks made were to be condensed into a single word, the word "goodness" would best represent it; for goodness expresses the very heart of his character and purposes. But for a description of his preaching and the direction in which both his preaching and his personal life thrust their influence the word would have to be "unity." He was the foremost spokesman of his day, not so much in specific argument and reasoned defense as in generous spirit and insight, for conceptions of God and nature and humanity which are commonplace now but were hardly so much as thought of by the religious orthodoxy which antedated him. He did not inaugurate the movement of these newer and more liberal ideas in his generation. Other men did that, particularly Horace

Bushnell, whom our generation has almost forgotten. At the memorial service after Brooks's death, his successor, Doctor Donald, said that Brooks's theology was "simply the theology of Bushnell." Brooks accepted the ideas; tested them in his own mind and life until they became part of the body of conviction by which he lived, and then preached them with such living, searching, responsive and happy eloquence that, as Bishop McDowell has said in one of his characteristic volumes, he left to all the churches a legacy of preachers scattered over the earth and revealing the influence of Brooks everywhere.

He was what every preacher who thinks deeply on his vocation desires to be, not a scholar nor a scientist nor a discoverer of new truth but an interpreter of whatever truth is discovered, in terms of life and experience, to those who otherwise would not or could not relate their religion to the changing world in which they lived. To paraphrase a penetrating characterization by Doctor Brastow, Brooks interpreted men to themselves, he told them things about themselves they did not know, he explained things of which they were only half conscious, he ennobled them in their own eyes, he interpreted the humanity of Christ and the divinity that is possible to men. Putting a dominant generalization into perhaps the most awkward language possible, he interpreted, first, the unity of the universe. That is not only a remarkably awkward phraseology but it expresses also a very commonplace truth; a truth which today is taken for granted while almost every disclosure of physical science confirms it. A book which within recent years has occasioned perhaps as much comment as any other in the deeper ranges of thought, is Professor Eddington's volume on *The Nature of the Physical World*. In it, through intricate scientific and mathematical discussions, he makes credible the conclusion that the fundamental reality is spirit. He followed that volume with another, the Swathmore Lecture on *Science and the Unseen World,* in which he declares his faith as a scientist in the reality of God as involved in the facts which his science discovers and with which it deals. Professor Eddington is not a theologian; he is a professor of astronomy in Cambridge University; and though Bertrand Russell has made a characteristic and hence destructive criticism upon it, the angels seem to be on the side of Eddington. This unity of the universe is an axiom with us.

It was not so when Phillips Brooks began to preach. It was an almost unknown conception well into the last half of the nineteenth century. Puritanism, Calvinism, Evangelicalism of all kinds; Congregationalists, Methodists, Baptists, Presbyterians, Episcopalians, all pulpits avowed, though they did not always realize the implication of their avowal, a divided universe. It was against this historic dualism that Bushnell had directed his revolutionary *Nature and the Supernatural.* There was the realm of matter and there was the realm of spirit. The stars above the earth were unrelated to it except in terms of distance and gravitation; so also God was remote from man, the spirit wholly apart from the flesh, the good from the bad. Theologians caught up Saint Paul's phrase in the fifteenth chapter of First Corinthians —"there is a natural body and there is a spiritual body"—and seemed to build whole systems on it. The natural man had nothing in common with the spiritual man. On earth there were only two kinds of people—the saints and the sinners, though the saints were, for the most part, saintly only by virtue of a divine imputation, not by achievement; and the saviours of the ark in all Protestant denominations were wrought into fever heat as late as 1899 by Borden P. Bowne's heretical declaration that there was a third kind—those who were tending in one direction or the other but who could not yet be authoritatively classified. The members of the church were presumably good, those not members of the church were at least not so good. The elect were saved, if one belonged to a foreordination faith; those not elect were reprobate and lost. Theology, that is to say, was not rooted in life, and the doctrines of religion could be kept altogether unrelated to the conduct of the men and women who most loyally believed them.

In the same way, though with more theological precision, Christ was curiously divided and discussed. There was the rather massive belief, massive in its historical background, that in Him were two natures wholly distinct yet indissolubly united —the divine nature and the human nature. When

Jesus hungered and slept and wept and suffered, that older theology said that it was by His human nature. When He foretold events and performed miracles, it was by His divine nature. He employed either as the occasion demanded and nevertheless with a slight variation from the New-Testament phrase, was held to be in all points like as we are yet without sin. Theology, having such a thesis, tried to distinguish between what He did and said as God and what He did and said as man; and Sunday-school teachers with the scantiest theological understanding and the most vague acquaintance with Scripture, attempted the same meticulous distinctions. Inevitably theories of the atonement, with all the sublimity which must always gather to the consideration of so profound and awesome a theme, were fearfully artificial, generally making the death of Christ and the salvation which men preached that He wrought by it as separate from the experience of men as any court procedure is from our daily life.

How these presumptions affected the outlook on human life is easily understood. Theology and the preachers who voiced the theology of the time, from the Puritans down to Phillips Brooks's day, and some of them, in fact, down into our own day, declared with David that all men were born in sin; that they were by birth the children of the devil; and that they had to be rescued from the devil and from the guilt of sin by the invasion of God into their lives. Evil and depravity were the natural condition of men, from birth; goodness was the divine, that is to say, their unnatural condition. The older forms of evangelism from Jonathan Edwards to Billy Sunday were based on this conception.

It was this theology of Calvinism and the Puritans into which Phillips Brooks was introduced and in which he was to a greater or less extent bred. To the end of his life, no Calvinist was more sure that God, as a theologian of our day puts it, was on the ground first. But Calvinism was not the theology which he preached; and to his preaching his generation owes the unstudied impetus which took it still farther from that older orthodoxy. Brooks preached what he personally had discovered, which was that it was not the world which was the reality and God a distant Spirit; but that God is the reality and, as Saint Paul had said, in Him we live, and move and have our being. He preached that the world is the expression of the presence and reality of God; that the entire universe—every thing, every creature, every mind—is organized to a common and eternal purpose, that far off divine event to which Tennyson declared the whole creation moves. But Brooks was certain that the unity was not merely in the future, it is also present here and now.

So he could not believe that Jesus was a divided, even though divinely divided, life. He could not believe in the two natures forever separated in the mechanical fashion of his time's traditional faith. Jesus was the disclosure, the revelation, the very incarnation of God; God made flesh; but not in any such divided condition as was suggested by the creed in which he had been brought up. He declared that it was just because the spiritual nature of man and the nature of God are a unity that men can recognize God. One of his definitive sayings was "We talk of men's reaching through nature up to nature's God"—which sounds like an echo of John Fiske: "It is nothing to the way in which they may reach through manhood up to manhood's God and learn the divine love by the human." "Because we are sons God hath sent forth the spirit of His son into our hearts."

Brooks held the incarnation as the very heart of life and history and, accordingly, nothing was farther from his conception of the atonement than the Calvinistic or the orthodox Arminian theories. Instead of God and Christ being outside the world of humanity he was sure of God and Christ inside this human world; and, like Bushnell before him, and Frederick Robertson, he proclaimed "a participation of man in the righteousness of God."

Very naturally, with Bushnell's idea of Christian nurture a part of his own body of conviction, he preached that children are born the children of God, not the children of the devil; they are born into the kingdom of God, not into the kingdom of sin. It is not God who must invade their world and rescue them; it is sin which first invades their world and imperils them. Sin, he contended, is the unnatural thing; the natural thing is goodness. His was, likewise, a modern conception of religion. It was a characteristically human endument, a man's possession, though I do not know that he used the precise word, not because he is good but because he is a man. Religion is not something conferred on a man when he becomes converted, because it is the normal man who is religious; it is the irreligious or unreligious man who is abnormal. Religion, as he put it, is but the highest conception of life.

All modern Christology is more or less vague, in comparison with the vigorous and hard outlines of earlier theologies; and Brooks's Christology was near the beginning of the modern lack of definiteness. One hesitates to pass inexpert judgment on this because it was the very definiteness of the older Christologies which defeated them. But while Brooks's Christology was vague, Christ was the center of his thinking, because, as with Samuel Rutherford two hundred and fifty years before, Christ was the center of his life. The evangelical piety in which he had been brought up from his childhood and through his university and seminary days alike, remained strong and rich and burgeoning, while the theology which was presumed to sustain it disintegrated in his mind.

It is to be expected, then, that while he knew more theology, as has been remarked, than appeared in his preaching, and claimed that productive preaching is always buttressed by Christian theology, his preaching was never technically theological. He took the position, as a student of his career has justly observed, that it is not the preacher's business either to criticize or to defend the theology of the Church. It is the preacher's business to declare the truth which his life and the life of man have discovered. Brooks's successor in the bishopric of Massachusetts, a friend who knew him intimately, explained this aspect of him by saying, "There was no scrap of his creed that did not have its vital relation with his life, and no little act of each day that did not have its vital relation with some of the deepest truths of his faith."

II

It would almost follow from what has already been said that a second element in the gospel which Phillips Brooks preached was tolerance. This does not mean the casual, glib, ready-to-wear tolerance which today makes the word so common and almost meaningless. With Brooks, as it should be with all others, it was rather a sober recognition of the rights of other people's mind without compromising his own in respect of those fundamental convictions which actually separated him from them. His biographer, Doctor Allen, in another connection suggests a truth to be taken into account here. For all of Brooks's insistence upon and love for intellectual freedom, Doctor Allen remarks that he became more and more certain that the real concern of the preacher should not be for liberty so much as for sympathy. It is a fruitful idea when carried through the consideration of Brooks's theological definiteness on the one hand, and catholicity of spirit on the other. Believing thoroughly, as he did, that only because men are essentially akin to God can they recognize the incarnation of God as it appears in the historic Jesus, Brooks could draw none of those hard and exclusive distinctions between men and men, between churches and churches, which were the habit of his day and have been the habit of the days since then.

Tolerance has become one of the catchwords of our generation, but for the most part it is a shoddy and blustering sort of tolerance which gives way easily in any hard weather of actual opposition. People repeat the word easily and often in proportion as they have neither opportunity for, nor understanding of what is involved in practicing it. It is too frequently a deceptive substitute for the difficulty of sound thought. There are not lacking those, in large numbers also, whose devotion to tolerance has in mind other people's and not their own. There are men and women today who make it almost the sole substance of their thinking and social speech; and who cannot see a political issue, a religious conviction, a social ideal, an industrial theory without bursting out into a demand for, or a complaint of, the lack of tolerance. One of the curious and amusing facts of contemporary experience is the number of these labeled liberals in pulpits and out of them who are so engaged with their obsession of tolerance that they are utterly intolerant of anyone who does not travel as far or in the same direction as they do. They are like the Philadelphia Quakers of whom John Adams wrote that they boasted of their plain clothes which cost much more than the fashionable garments of their neighbors, and were positively proud of their humility.

The reason that at least some of these almost professionally tolerant folks are what they are is that they have no great, commanding convictions on which they build and sustain their lives. No minister but can recall Christians who have told him that they do not believe in foreign missions because other races are satisfied with their own religions, and why, they ask, should we disturb them by taking Christianity to them? Sometimes they vary their objection by assuring the minister patronizingly that all religions are going on to the same God anyway. One risks no denial in saying that to such Christians Christianity means very little which Christ would recognize as from Himself. Such Christians are either uninformed of Christianity's contribution to the world during its nineteen centuries of history or are shutting their eyes to facts which, if acknowledged, would challenge their conscience. Certainly, they are untouched by its recreative and constraining power. It is a growing fashion to declare that the differences between Catholicism and Protestantism can be ignored in the light of the increasing practical agreements between Catholics and Protestants. That is not tolerance but sheer ignorance to which real tolerance is impossible. What divides Protestantism from Catholicism is not any difference in personal character or spiritual desire on the part of Catholics and Protestants. It is not a matter of forms and altars, of celibate priests and married clergy. It is a vitally different conception of life, of history, of the Scriptures, of the Church, of government and society, of the world, of the function of intelligence itself. All the friendliness, the social harmony, the personal admiration and affection and good will which, on an enlarging scale, obtain between modern Catholics and Protestants do not and cannot alter that difference so as to make any fundamental compromise possible for an understanding mind on either side. This is not a matter of tolerance or intolerance; it is a matter of characteristic and essential insight. People can be really and constructively tolerant only as they have certain deep, immovable convictions which they have to hold against the world if need be; and those who claim to be tolerant when they have nothing over which they can be honestly intolerant do not know the meaning of the word. As one of the most luminous minds of the last generation said, tolerance is founded not upon the uncertainty but upon the certainty of truth.

Phillips Brooks was certain of the truth; not that he had all of it, but that anything which men anywhere had found to be true was worthy of reverence. His distinctive question when he faced any new challenge to thought or experience, any difference of judgment on things thought or experienced, was not, Is it orthodox? as most of his contemporaries asked, but, Is it true? He believed in the Christian doctrine of the Trinity, for instance; yet in his preaching he did not criticize any formulation of it nor defend it from any current criticism. For him, personally, it was a reliable statement of the riches of the nature and the grace of God which he could appropriate. He could not quarrel with another man for whom it was not such a statement.

Archbishop Temple, in his *The Universality of Christ,* somewhere reports his opinion that one of the gains of our generation has been the recognition of the duty of reverence for other men's beliefs. But he adds the caution that reverence for other men's beliefs does not mean acceptance of them. It means to recognize that whatever thoughts any human soul is seeking to live by deserve the reverence of every other soul. Phillips Brooks came at a period when that was by no means the general rule of religious attitudes or conduct. The two-hundred-year-old Puritan tradition, the New-England theology which it maintained, recognized no such inclusiveness of truth. That might possibly have been the unexpressed, perhaps unformulated, feeling of the rank and file of the Christians who constituted the membership of the churches, though even that is doubtful; but it was not the official expression of either theology or ecclesiasticism, of pulpit theologians or pulpit ecclesiastics. They maintained the old exclusiveness in judgment. You were of the elect or you were not; you were converted in a definite and

—at least inwardly—dramatic experience or you were not; you were properly confirmed or you were not; you were immersed or you were not. And if you were not, the covenant mercies of God had not been extended to you.

Phillips Brooks in his pulpit, not by theological arguments but by the lucid exposition of goodness which he made so natural and attractive; by the sheer magnetism of his personal character and the ethical clarity of his mind; by the contagion of spiritual reality kindled in his personal contacts went far to break that stubborn position. He was an Episcopalian, body, mind, and soul, and could not have been at home in any other Communion. He was unalterably a believer in the Trinity, and Unitarianism was impossible for him. But the very strength of his own commitments and loyalties gave him resources of tolerance the expression of which was perhaps his greatest social contribution to the temper of his time. "He had such confidence in his own faith in Christ that he had no hesitation in recognizing . . . any ray of truth from whatever source it came. He believed so firmly in his Church, her creeds and standards, that he was confident she would with him welcome truth from the agnostic, the Calvinist, the Unitarian or any other truthseeker." He discovered at one time that he was somewhat mistaken, when he was being voted for a Bishop of Massachusetts and his eulogy of the character and faith of James Freeman Clarke, a great Unitarian leader, was urged against his election. Also, the opposition charged, he had participated in a union Good-Friday service in a Congregational church.

He remains one of our greatest creditors in the things of the spirit. His preaching, his books, his personal character led in that movement of thought and life which carried nineteenth-century Protestantism in America away from the hard, rigid, theological, intolerant New-England tradition into the practical and fraternal Protestantism of today. He was not a scholar; he made no contribution to knowledge. But he believed that the instinctive beliefs of the sincere and reverent spirit will ultimately be more sustaining than what have been called the pride of dogma and the distractions of dispute.

III

In the discussion so far what has been indicated is not so much Phillips Brooks's influence as what lay back of his influence. He preached his conviction of the kinship of God and man, the divine unity of the whole realm of intellectual and moral life; but whatever he did for men's thinking they did not go from Trinity Church saying to themselves that they must now believe in that particular fashion. He proclaimed tolerance, by speech and manner, declared for it in public address and printed page; but those who heard and read him did not respond by saying to themselves or to others that now they intended to be tolerant. People heard Phillips Brooks and went away determined that they were going to be good. Brooks illustrated his own theories of preaching, particularly that the chief requirement for the preacher was not that he should have liberty but that he should have and exemplify sympathy. He made his congregations sure that goodness was worthwhile, that it was a livable and reasonable enterprise in a rather difficult but inspiring world. Brooks subscribed completely to Bushnell's luminous remark that "loving God is but letting God love us." One of the deep and characteristic impressions which he left on sensitive spirits was of the way in which, as someone has phrased it, "he carried the Eternal as a living force in his life." It is obvious that the only way in which anyone can give that impression to his contemporaries is by a personal goodness, a personal breadth and magnanimity and clarity, so real and inescapable that men think of the Eternal whenever he comes.

It is here that Phillips Brooks has perhaps the most important meaning for the ministry of today. For a generation in America there has been a great insistence on the part of Christian laymen that their ministers shall be good mixers, and good sports, and regular fellows, and the like; and presumably that sort of minister has some advantages in the matter of personal contacts and social popularity which everyone might covet. But with all the obsolete language and the stiffness of the past to which we would not want to return, it is not greatly to be doubted that the churches and Christian life in America would be better off today if for a generation the laymen had found and made their preachers men of God. And this is not a reflection concerning ministers only. We have come a long way from the austerity of the Puritan religion, from the exclusiveness of Jonathan Edwards, from the impassioned revolutionary experience of Whitefield, and look back to them and their religious conceptions as stages in the progress of religion which we have passed. But when we have called them stages now left behind, it still remains true that the men and women of those more austere beliefs were sure of their way. It may have been a dark way, and hard; it may have left too little place for laughter, too small a room in which the soul could sing; though the austerity of the sterner generations is probably heightened by perspective out of all proportion to the reality. But it was a straight way and the men and women who walked it knew their direction and had no doubt of their goal. That was what their religion, stern as it may have been, did for them; which is what religion ought to do at all times; and is precisely what, for the most part, it is not doing for men and women today.

Instead of what seems to us, as we look back, to have been the straight and direct road on which our fathers walked, we are set down where many paths cross, and the ground before us is covered and confused with footprints that point in all directions. We are perplexed and hesitant, with every magazine editor, discontented social worker, dismissed preacher, and dilettante critic asking whether we do not need a new religion, or expounding some new form of faith to be established amid the debris of the old. And there are also these half-provocative, half-fascinating prophets piecing together the fragments of wrecked philosophies salvaged from the past which found them wanting, who invite us to join them in the satisfactions offered by their strange gospel that they do not know where they are going but are on the way.

In a day vocal with political admonitions, social theories, and the slogans of emergency agencies of government; a day in which one of the fundamental needs of the Christian pulpit is a rediscovery of what constitutes the essential gospel, the preacher needs to remember that there remains one unmistakable re-enforcement for a confused world. That is the re-enforcement of personal goodness actually operating in social relationships; the radiance of personal character conducting itself in the things and occasions of time so nobly that, as in Phillips Brooks, the Eternal is recognized as a living force. The fundamental criticism of Christianity today, if the various indictments of the ministry were synthesized, would be that it has lost its radiance. Men who can remember Brooks, Henry Drummond, Maltbie D. Babcock, have no difficulty in realizing the difference between them and the ministry of today, though they have no criticism either of the character, the devotion or the intellectual life of the present-day ministry. The indefinable quality of

E. Stanley Jones is not in any extraordinary intellectual force or studied eloquence. It is in a radiance which may defy definition but makes itself unmistakably known through personal contact as well as public utterance.

That radiance was not so general that Brooks's emanation of it could seem commonplace. The old way of being good was hard and the radiant spirits disclosed the hardness the more vividly. It was a matter of rigid practices, of heroic renunciation, of very constant impoverishment of many aspects of life, so that one reads the tale of Puritan and Covenanter and earlier Methodist and Hardshell Baptist with increasing admiration for their fortitude and devotion but with commensurate regret for the narrowness which excluded from their lives so much of loveliness and worth. Scotland's faith could have been just as glorious and not so sterile of beauty if John Knox had not been blinded to the beautiful by his dedication to implacable righteousness. Methodism in generations past could have been just as impassioned, just as transforming, just as militant and sure, and not barren for so many years of art and social graces, if its dominant spirits had been open to the truths that lie in other realms than those of religious experience and theology.

Today a confused generation needs in every sphere of life and relationship the impact of men and women whose personal characters are so impressive that their kinship with the Eternal cannot be escaped. What men and women are looking for now is something of which they can be sure. The one thing of which they can be sure, the one thing in which they cannot help believing, is the creative witness of a truly good life; a life not partial and intolerant and harsh in the goodness of a great though unamiable conviction, but rich and satisfying and compelling, sure of its faith and hope while reverencing the rights of those whose faith and hope take quite other forms. The child of the trite old anecdote who prayed that the bad people might be made good and the good people nice had hit upon the foremost duty of contemporary Christians, the duty of making goodness attractive not by compromising it but by irradiating it with beauty of the Eternal. In that duty Phillips Brooks can still show the way.

The Impatient Parson, a few years ago, had recovered the principle upon which modern Christianity needs greatly to act. "It is no new definition of religion that is required, but a new realization of it."[1] The most vital revival of religion, as he also suggested, and the one most needed today, is not one that will change men from unbelief to belief, but from more belief to realization. It is a great deal easier, even in a day of revolutionary changes in theology, to believe the older doctrines of Christianity of which we are now getting rid, than it is to practice the actual meaning of Christianity of which we dare never get rid if we are to be Christians at all.

Dr. E. Stanley Jones tells the story of a mis-

[1] Sheppard: *The Impatience of a Parson,* p. 25.

sionary who, while giving a Bible lesson in a zenana, observed one of the Hindu ladies going out, and later returning. At the close of the meeting the missionary asked her why she went out, was she not interested? "Oh, yes, I was so interested in the wonderful things you were saying that I went out to ask your carriage driver whether you really meant it and whether you lived it at home. He said you did, so I came back to listen again."[2]

That was the Word—as Carlyle's robust habit of using capitals would indicate—of Phillips Brooks to his generation. Religion, he knew, has to be theological, but it is more than theology; it is theology made flesh and dwelling among us. He, particularly of the preachers of his day, carried religion out of theology into the experience of life; and behind his leadership American Protestanism has learned that life is more than theological meat, and the body of a living experience and character more than denominational raiment.

References

Allen, A. V. G., *Phillips Brooks, 1835-1893.*
Brastow, L. O., *Representative Modern Preachers.*
Clarke, W. Newton, *Huxley and Phillips Brooks.*
Farrar, Dean F. W., *Men I Have Known.*
Gordon, George A., *My Education and My Religion.*
Lawrence, Bishop William, *Phillips Brooks.*
Potter, Bishop Henry C., *Reminiscences of Bishops and Archbishops.*

[2] E. Stanley Jones: *The Christ of the Round Table,* p. 130.

VIII

GEORGE A. GORDON: THE MAGNIFICENT REBEL

VIII

GEORGE A. GORDON: THE MAGNIFICENT REBEL

In the history of any sustained movement of thought or faith progress is registered not only in the orderly evolution of ideas, but also, from time to time, by events common enough in themselves but in their particular time and circumstance critical and decisive. In the disintegration of the New-England theology, the central figure of such a critical and decisive event was George A. Gordon.

His name brings to any mind at all acquainted with the American pulpit the figure of the man who, more than any other in the past century, represented that pulpit at its best. For Gordon, to an extent unequaled by any of his contemporaries, combined profound scholarship, encyclopedic knowledge, spiritual insight, precise logic, and pulpit eloquence. At the same time he was not lacking in those simplicities and sympathies which put his highest qualities at the service of the humblest personal life. If one were compelled to name the two men of modern time without whom the history of New-England religious thought and its dissolution into liberalism cannot be explained, he would find himself eventually mentioning Horace Bushnell and George A. Gordon, whom John Wright Buckham has called our third great theologian. Jonathan Edwards, of course, was the first, though there might be differences of opinion as to the identity of the second. Doctor Buckham, naming one after another a group of American thinkers each of whom perhaps in some one particular aspect surpassed Gordon, ends a paragraph of appraisal by saying that nevertheless, in insight and breadth and total accomplishment, none has equaled him.[1]

Over the world of literature and history, of philosophy and science he ranged with ease and from it all gathered almost illimitable materials with which to illustrate and clothe his thought. From the time that he was twenty-four years of age until he was seventy-three, he was a Congregational minister in the active and actual pastorate of three churches; giving to the last, for generations one of the truly great churches of America, forty-two years of uninterrupted service. During the same time he was Preacher to Harvard University for nine years, Preacher to Yale University for twenty-eight years; delivered series after series of important lectures at Yale, Harvard, and the Lowell Institute; was an Overseer at Harvard for seven years, a trustee of Andover for ten; while the books of permanent value which he wrote would in themselves constitute a life's work. Saying nothing of his pulpit style, the unsurpassed form and manner and beauty of his utterances, but thinking chiefly of the mind of the man, two

[1] *Progressive Religious Thought in America,* p. 87.

things alone would mark him as one of the gigantic figures of the modern Church. First, he was a master of, utterly at home in, the whole history of theology from the early Christian Fathers to the present time—an intellectual achievement not expected of anyone except a specialist in that particular field. Second, he was equally supreme in the field of philosophy. It has been said of him by one competent to know, that if the references to Plato in his writings were to be put together, they would themselves make a volume. But not Plato alone; the systems of Aristotle, Fichte, Kant, Hegel, Hume, and one after another, the insights and conclusions of other philosophical minds were familiar country to him. As an illustration of his sheer scholarship the incident is told that when he and a friend one day were disputing about a point in Plato's *Republic,* Doctor Gordon took out of his pocket a small copy of Plato in the original Greek, an old and well-worn copy, and turned at once to the passage.

I

With all this forbidding scholarship, the outstanding feature of the man was his friendly humanness; and the story of his life, if the limits of a chapter permitted it, would be a story of common sense and laughter and simple reality. Some of that story should be told, on the way to his meaning for our day and us, and to begin at the beginning is to say that he was born in Scotland on January 2, 1853. His father was an overseer of an estate, a man of humble circumstances but with all the noblest Scotch qualities of industry and honor; his mother a woman who could have been remarkable in any sphere of life. When young George Gordon was married in this country, he sent a cablegram to his mother and in time received her letter in reply. It reveals her mind and character though there were only three sentences in it. She wrote:

My Dear Son:

I would like to send a few words of thanks, for all your great kindness to me, especially for the cablegram. I knew by that, that you smiled on me. In the light of thy countenance is life!

Ever your loving mother,

Catherine Gordon.

In his father's home, Doctor Gordon has written in his autobiography, "Calvinism was the perfect philosophy of the Old and New Testament, the last word about God and the meaning of man's life."[2] And the one great fault which he says he found with his ancestors, looking at them from the point of view of his boyhood, was that they were all too fond of work and too religious. He was only a boy when that Calvinism began to trouble him, and he put the question to his mother, "If I should try all my life to be good, do you think I would get to heaven?"

And she said, "No, not if predestination is against you; many are called, but few are chosen."

[2] Gordon: *My Education and Religion*, p. 15.

Then he changed it and asked, "If I should try with all my might, all my life, to do my duty in the love of God, do you think that I should get into heaven?"

And she answered again, "No; many are called, but few are chosen; unless you are elected, there is no hope."

"Then," said he, "I am done with religion. I am not going to throw away both worlds. I am going to have a good time here and take what comes to me there."[3]

He grew up in the way an average Scotch boy would grow up, disciplined harshly at times, working, going to school in the older school life of that day. There were certain unmistakable loyalties. He was taught to lift his hat to three persons, the minister who took care of the souls of the community, the doctor who took care of their bodies, and the schoolmaster who took care of their minds. But they had some irreverences as well. When he was seven and a brother eleven, they were sent together to the school, with a note from their father which read:

DEAR MR. DUNN:

I am sending my boys to your excellent school. They are very wild boys. Will you be especially severe with them.

The "wild boys," aged seven and eleven, buried the note under a stone which they took out of the stone fence by the road; and twenty-four years

[3] Gordon: *My Education and Religion,* p. 69f.

later the same two brothers spent many hours hunting in the stones of the fence to recover the note; but time and weather had been too much for it.

In his day at home religion was the main concern, work the next; and the Sabbath symbolized it all. It was kept, Doctor Gordon recalls, as if it had been the Jews' and not the Christians' religious day. "It was a duty," he says, "to penalize oneself, one's family, one's friends; it was a duty to be intolerant and even censorious in regard to all who might differ in opinion as to how the Sabbath ought to be kept."[4] And he adds a story, which he says is true to life, of a young man who had broken the letter of the law of Sabbath keeping and defended himself with the remark that the Lord allowed His disciples to rub the ears of corn in their hands and eat them on the Sabbath; and was answered at once by the old lady who was rebuking him, who said, "Aye, I ken that, and to tell ye the truth, I never thought any the better of the dear Lord for his behaviour on that day."[5] The whole business of Sabbath was the church, walking from two to six miles each way; sitting, in winter in a building without a stove, on narrow wooden seats with high straight backs, and listening to very long sermons on immense and complicated Calvinistic themes, the only part of which the boys could ever understand was that about the everlasting punishment of the

[4] Gordon: *My Education and Religion,* p. 109.
[5] *Ibid.,* p. 110.

wicked. Here, Gordon says, the preacher was dealing with the class to which he belonged.

When he was eighteen, this young Gordon sailed in the steerage for the United States, and discovered that fifty years ago a jail sentence of two weeks was nothing in comparison with two weeks in the steerage. He came with a sister, sailing up the Saint Lawrence to Quebec, and leaving Quebec on a hot summer night, for Boston. He saw sparks of light in the grass as the train ran on, and having been told that the country was full of snakes he thought these lights were snakes' eyes winking. He learned later that they were fireflies. When they changed to the Grand Trunk line, the cars were so much finer than anything they had ever seen before that they did not dare go inside, but decided to try it because they could only be ordered out; and when they learned that they were in the right train and need not change till they got to Boston, he says it was a joy to step from hell to heaven. He got a cup of tea which he thought was poisoned, and then learned that it was the kind of which American ladies were fond. In Boston he hunted work and found it, building burglarproof safes, working as a stonemason, painting doors and vaults, and helping to edit a monthly paper called *The Cherub* which, he said, long ago returned to heaven.

One's temptation is to linger too long over the incidents of his life and so lose the purpose of the chapter, which is not to exploit the man but to recognize his message and to apply it to our own religious life and time. So that suddenly now, passing over the human incidents and influences, the struggles and mistakes and hardships, the books bought at second-hand stores with terribly hard-earned money, he is to be seen at twenty-one entering the theological seminary, graduating three years later; ordained in his first church, in a very small community, seven miles and a half from the jumping-off place of the single-track railroad, with many people in it who had never been on the train and could not be persuaded to get on one. But people, they were, rich in character, faith and affection. The next year, reversing the order of things, he entered Harvard University and graduated with honors in philosophy, in three years. At once he was installed minister of the Congregational Church in Greenwich, Connecticut; and three years later was the minister of the Old South Congregational Church, Boston.

II

So voluminous a writer and so penetrating and profound a thinker cannot be represented in a brief chapter, but Doctor Gordon's characteristic service to modern Christian doctrine through more than forty years of distinguished ministry can be suggested. What gifts of robust and wide-ranging thought were not native to him he inherited from the great stream of philosophy and theology which he had made his own, and from Bushnell, whose "vein of comprehensiveness" represents the very quality of Gordon's mind. While he was rich in emotions and sympathies, his religious assurance came to him through the march of magnificent and logical intelligence, and his emotion, as far as it was an expression of religion, was always the product of thought. As he himself has related, he found himself on the road to his own certainties during his years at Harvard when he reached the conviction that the truths of religion, like those of science, must be truths reached and tested by reason. From this he advanced, during his first pastorate, to the position from which the New-England theology could not defend itself, that the only basis of a conviction able to survive the inexorable criticisms of the reason, is experience. He put the truth in his *Ultimate Conceptions of Faith,* writing that "The soul in Christian experience, resting upon God and upon his discipline, is the great generative source of the convictions that support the highest work of the world."[6]

Bushnell restored Christ to the center of American theology. Brooks, of course, had no other thought of it. But it was Gordon, not Bushnell, who restated the case in convincing terms and in terms perhaps as final as anything can be in the variable continuities of theology. "We are compelled to acknowledge that the secret molding energy of our entire civilization is in the mind of Christ."[7]

---

[6] *Op. cit.,* p. 92.

[7] "Some Things Worthwhile in Theology," *Harvard Theological Review,* III, No. 4, p. 51.

It is probably true, as criticism has asserted, that Gordon fails to distinguish adequately between the Jesus of history and the Christ of faith; and no one aware of the distance traveled by the present day in its demand for the social application and experience of religion will think that Gordon realized how radical the present social demands on Christianity are. But this failure to discriminate clearly between the Christ of faith and Jesus was a defect of Bushnell's and has been repeated generally, while when the large number of contemporary theologians, preachers, and religious-minded laymen who have not yet realized the social responsibilities of religion is recognized, Doctor Gordon is hardly to be condemned for not taking more advanced ground forty years ago.

He replaced the inconsistencies of the New-England theology's conception of God and the more sentimental alternatives to it with a conception morally invulnerable and logically triumphant. His conclusions were unorthodox and would be so considered in many quarters today. He argued that the moral opportunity of men is not confined to this life; that if this is a moral world, the Creator's redeeming interest in mankind must continue forever; that the question is not what men deserve but what God's honor demands. "The Absolute Will is absolute in goodness; therefore the deduction that God is on the side of some men and against others is an illogical deduction."[8]

[8] *Ultimate Conceptions of Faith,* p. 26.

The conclusion of his theology of salvation is hardly short of universalism, but is wholly inclusive. It is that "God's love and endeavor are for all his children and for them all forever."[9]

Some of the most significant phases of Gordon's thinking must necessarily be left unmentioned, but his treatment of miracles must be remarked. It appears completely in his Nathaniel W. Taylor lectures at Yale in 1909. The essence of them can be fairly crushed into his own sentence that, "the unverifiable can never remain an essential part of reasonable faith."[10] On that premise he argues that it is immaterial how Jesus came into the world and how he was raised from the dead; what is significant is simply that Jesus came and that now we have the assurance of a risen Lord. That the volume awakened a storm of criticism is not astonishing. It would do so today if it were read by some religious groups. His own spirit amid the tempest appears in a letter to a friend:

> I am getting a terrible pounding from all over the country, . . . and from some good men whom I deeply respect and truly love. Since it is said that "the way of the transgressor is hard," and that "the way of the prophet is hard," I am not quite sure which way I am on. I think, however, that I am following the *Gleam.*[11]

The phrase is spiritually photographic. When one is moved by the majestic eloquence of Gor-

[9] *The New Epoch for Faith,* p. 278.
[10] *Religion and Miracles,* p. 38.
[11] Ct. Buckham, *Progressive Religious Thought,* p. 118f.

don's speech, subdued by the magnificence of the body of his thought and the sweep of his compelling knowledge, and captured by the precisions of his reason, one has nevertheless the feeling that the orator, the theologian, the advocate, is yet most truly a follower of the Gleam. Those who today enjoy the more humane and tolerant religious beliefs which have become common and productive among us may never have heard of him but they are in his debt.

III

This constructive and, at the time, revolutionary contribution which Gordon rendered the cause of liberal theology was not, however, his distinctive and supreme service, significant as it has been and disturbing as it was at the time. It was, rather, a service made possible, or at least made effective, by the success he won dramatically and in a single evening, in the most critical episode of his experience. Bushnell's great ministry was through his books. Brooks wrought out his share in the progress of liberal religion through many years of pulpit and pastoral ministry. But Gordon, whose books surpass Bushnell's in number, content, and circulation, and whose pulpit and pastoral ministry extended over a longer period than that of Brooks and commanded even more serious intellectual respect, achieved the great and fructifying accomplishment, which initiated his lifelong theological service and gave it both possibility and power, in one brief, critical, and courageous adventure of conviction which brought to an end the reign of the New-England theology and consolidated liberal Protestant thought in America in a position from which, within fifty years, it has won practically universal acceptance. That adventure of conviction was at his installation as minister of the Old South Church.

Installing a minister, to most of us, would appear to be a very formal and not particularly important event; interesting to the minister involved in it, and offering a social and religious opportunity to the congregation, but not specially significant in the larger matters of faith and life. But installing George A. Gordon into the pastorate of the Old South Congregational Church, Boston, in 1884, was one of the determining incidents for a generation's religious belief and development. First of all, we have to remember that the minister's relation to the church, in Congregationalism, is not quite like the relation of the minister to the church in any other denomination; or perhaps it would be better to say that it is like the relation of the minister to the church in very few other denominations. The relation of a Methodist preacher to his church, for illustration, is rather slight—apart from the circumstance of being temporarily the minister. He does not belong to his church; he has no contract of any kind with the church; there is normally no guarantee given him by the church as to the length of his stay there, and none given by him or by anyone else as to how long he will remain, and in the very few instances in which such unusual contract exists, time generally demonstrates its futility. He is appointed to his church annually, and the appointment is only for one year, and does not even then carry with it the necessity that he shall stay for the whole year. A Methodist minister belongs to the Methodist Episcopal ministry as a whole; he is a minister of the denomination, and is related to it through his membership in whichever Annual Conference he happens to be. He takes upon himself the vows of the ministry, pledges himself to certain loyalties of belief and character and conduct, not to, or in the presence of any specific church society, but before some Annual Conference of ministers, representing Methodism as a whole. There is a body of doctrine to which all Methodists hold. It is susceptible of very liberal and diverse interpretations, and it would now be almost impossible to have a heresy trial in the Methodist Church; but all Methodist preachers look to a common body of a few essential and determining beliefs, so that when the committee of a church expresses a desire to have any minister come to its pulpit, no one then and no one later asks him what he believes; it is taken for granted that he is somewhere reasonably safe within the circumference of our denominational theology. This statement finds rare exceptions in cases in which very ardent conservatives, either theological or economic, inquire into the attitude of the preacher toward their convictions; but in general the statement is within the truth. Furthermore, as the Methodist preacher is appointed to the church by the Bishop, only a Bishop can remove him, except in the case of misconduct unfitting him for the pastorate, when the Bishop's representative, the District Superintendent, suspends him until the whole matter has been investigated; and then, if the evidence warrants it, he is brought to trial—but not before the church of which he is the minister. The church would have nothing to do with it except as some of its members might be called as witnesses. Only a group of ministers selected from the Conference can try him. His essential relations in belief and character, in other words, are not with a local church, even though he is its minister, but with the Methodist Episcopal Church as a whole. That is why, contrary to a good deal of opinion, Methodist ministers as a class are perhaps the most independent ministers in America. If they are hard-pressed in one place, they know there is a city of refuge somewhere to which they may flee from the avenger.

But it is otherwise with Congregational and other independent churches. A Congregational minister's relations are with the church of which he is minister. It examines and satisfies itself as to his theology; it makes and ends his relations with it subject to the confirmation of the local Council; and between him and the church there exists the substance of a mutual contract. So that when fifty years ago a Congregational church installed a pastor it was a very decisive event for the church; and it happened that when the Old South Church, in 1884, gathered, through its officials, to install George A. Gordon, it was a very decisive event for the New-England religious tradition.

There were sixty-six men, some ministers but mostly laymen, in the Council which examined him prior to the service of installation. The program called for an examination of the young minister, which was expected to take perhaps an hour; then a rather elaborate supper for the Council and some invited guests; then some addresses of welcome to the new minister and a greeting extended by Phillips Brooks; Professor Tucker was to preach and another prominent minister would give an address to the people of South Church; and so everyone would have a pleasant time and go home about ten o'clock. The Council met at five-thirty; supper was set for six-thirty; but when six-thirty came there was no Council come out of its secret chamber and the supper was delayed. It was delayed until no one could wait any longer, and the invited guests sat down by themselves. The speeches that were supposed to be made to the Council and the new minister were made with no minister or Council present; and then when everyone wondered what had happened, at nine o'clock the Council came out to find only cold fragments of a devastated supper, with the report that there had been forty-eight votes in favor of the minister and eighteen against him. They heard Doctor Tucker's sermon and the other address, the minister was installed, feeling, he said, as if the whole South Church were sitting on his breast; and the small blizzard that was raging outside was no colder than the spiritual temperature Doctor Gordon felt within.

There had been liberal revolts in New-England Councils before this, and there had been some successful revolts, though neither the number of revolts nor the number of liberal successes had been such as confidently determined the future. In the fall of 1877 a Rev. James F. Merriam was invited to become the minister of the Congregational church in Indian Orchard, a factory suburb of Springfield, Massachusetts. He was a man of singularly fine spirit and glorious unselfishness, of which he had given thorough evidence during a year in which he had been the acting pastor before being called to the pulpit. He was refused installation, after a notable controversy, because he would neither believe nor declare that those who die unrepentant suffer eternally. He leaned toward what we now call conditional immortality. A few weeks after he had been denied installation Theodore T. Munger was before another Council which was interrogating him in order to determine whether he should be installed in the Congregational pulpit at North Adams. His orthodoxy was challenged at several points, particularly at this same point of disbelief in unconditional and eternal punishment. Munger was more vigorous and varied in his unorthodoxy than Merriam, but he was far more skillful, though never specious or insincere, in his own defense, and he was installed, though with a powerful minority against him. Neither of these incidents greatly affected contemporary theology. But when the night came to an end on which George A. Gordon was installed as a minister of the Old South Church the old New-England theology which had weathered many a storm since the time of Jonathan Edwards, though battered here and there by some protesting soul, was in collapse; for the rebellion of Gordon and his election to the pulpit of that great church in spite of it, spelled the doom of the old system.

What happened behind those closed doors was what always took place in much the same fashion when a minister was thus examined. He was asked every sort of question concerning his belief, particularly his belief in the New-England Calvinistic system of theology. Some of the questions and answers were not always without humor. One such preacher had been tricked into saying that the sinner has a part in his own conversion, which, of course, the New-England system would not have. Immediately one of the questioners asked him, "What part? Did the man with the withered hand, whom Jesus healed, have any part in the healing?" And the young minister replied, "Yes, he had a hand in it." Another question asked was the traditional inquiry whether the minister being examined was willing to be damned for the glory of God.

This question is not as ridiculous as it might appear to be. If one believes that it is the will of

God for some to be damned, he ought to be as willing to be damned himself as that anyone else should be, since he should be devoted to the will of God. Whatever the will of God should involve, ought in a consistent Calvinist, to be met by a willingness on the part of the believer. At this point, however, conscience comes in conflict with theology if the believer is thoughtful enough to discover the conflict. As Professor Douglas Clyde Macintosh has put it:

> A man who could seriously set himself the duty of being disinterested enough to be willing to be damned for the glory of God was a much more moral being than a God who could for his own glory eternally damn men who, because of original sin, were unable to repent and gain salvation.[12]

And on one occasion the minister who had been badgered over the whole sweep of Calvinism answered that he was not willing to be damned for the glory of God, but if it were for the glory of God that the Council questioning him should be damned, he would raise no objection.

Here then, on a memorable night, is George A. Gordon, a young minister, thirty-one years old, with only a few years' experience but with a profound education and profound intelligence, a deep piety and much courage, being examined as to his loyalty to a system of belief from which he had turned away. The Council found him orthodox and happily satisfactory on the question of God,

[12] M. H. Krumbine (Editor): *Process of Religion*: A symposium, p. 105.

and the Person of Jesus, the Holy Spirit and the Bible, and on matters of salvation, of religion, and conduct. But he denied the New-England scheme of atonement and denied the everlasting punishment of the wicked. He said that to affirm that God was absolute goodness and then to declare that God as absolute goodness would arbitrarily elect some men to eternal reprobation and some to eternal salvation, was a supreme instance of bad logic. It illustrates the artificiality of that once great and vital theology that these good men, who acknowledged Gordon's loyalty to all that the New Testament imposes, and who knew the richness of his personal character, were far more concerned for that system than for the truth. As Gordon himself wrote of it, "The gospel of Jesus might be affirmed, but that did not count, because it could not take care of itself; it was impotent without the guardianship of the New-England Calvinism."[13] When Gordon denied the everlasting punishment of the wicked, the preacher who presided and had agreed to make the prayer at the installation, withdrew his consent to pray; and the eighteen others cast their votes against the young minister. The vote even then could have been made unanimous in Gordon's favor if the forty-eight had been willing to make some compromising statement; but they said: "No. This man believes in God, the Father of Jesus Christ, and he believes in the program of Jesus for the help and salvation of man, and is going in on his

[13] Gordon: *My Education and Religion,* p. 233.

record, New-England theology to the contrary, notwithstanding."[14] It might have seemed to be just a local Boston affair, but within the year the installation of other ministers on that simple, sound theology where formerly they would have been rejected, witnessed that the old system was gone. George A. Gordon, thirty-one years old, dared to thrust the sincerity of a new spiritual insight against the bulwarked theology which for two hundred and fifty years had stood against every antagonism, and the theology went down, while over its ruins a new generation's simpler, freer, more hopeful, more brotherly, more New Testament-like faith came in.

Of course this one minister did not do it all by himself. He followed, at the culminating time, a line of theological rebels who, before him, had begun the attack and made the campaign. But for Gordon to have failed would have meant a serious repulse to liberalism. Of course his installation in Old South Church was not his final contribution to the liberal movement. He had forty-two years in his pulpit there. What Brooks was doing at Trinity Church by his prophetic goodness and the inspiration of a preaching that declared the truth without arguing it, Gordon established in the region of the intellect and developed through such thoughtful, sustaining, effective preaching as few churches have heard and few men have accomplished.

[14] Gordon: *My Education and Religion,* p. 230.

References

Book of the Fortieth Year . . . Fortieth Anniversary of the Installation of George A. Gordon as Minister of the Old South Church in Boston (1924).

Buckham, J. W., *Progressive Religious Thought in America.*

Gordon, G. A., *My Education and Religion: An Autobiography.*

Our Heritage, Old South Church, 1669-1919.

The Congregationalist (Boston), November 14, 21; December 12, 1929.

IX

WASHINGTON GLADDEN AND APPLIED CHRISTIANITY

IX

WASHINGTON GLADDEN AND APPLIED CHRISTIANITY

"THE story which I have undertaken to tell," so Washington Gladden begins his *Recollections,* "is that of an average American," a remark which deserves special attention because it is probably the only untruth he ever told. "It holds no such wonders of achievement as that of Booker T. Washington; it follows no such romantic paths as those in which Jacob Riis has led us; it climbs to no such altitudes of dignity and power as those to which we have rejoiced to follow Carl Schurz."[1] These comparisons are true; but not to the disparaging inference which Doctor Gladden seems to wish drawn, for he was not an average American. There is an element of wonder in his achievements. There is something of romance in his Odyssey from a New York farm to the forefront of the liberal pulpit in America, and one cannot contemplate the position which he held so long in American opinion, and the influences which he set in motion, without very clear sight of altitudes both of dignity and power.

There might seem to be no connection between him and the New-England theology with which this volume has somewhat to do; for he was born in Pennsylvania and his mother was a girl from

[1] *Op. cit.,* p. 1.

the state of New York. But New England was strong in his blood if not in his theology, although even there his connection is direct. His father was born in Massachusetts of an old New-England family, the boy's paternal grandfather being a Connecticut Yankee, and before him the family was New England back to Old England itself. In early childhood the boy spent a year in his grandfather's home, from which daily he looked up to Mount Tom. His college was a New-England college, and two of his pastorates were in New-England communities. Theologically he was a New Englander though of a philosophical lineage little applauded east of the Hudson, being a spiritual son of Horace Bushnell, whose "heresy" he accepted because, as he said years later, it was from Bushnell that he learned the only doctrine he could preach.

He was born in 1836, and his father, a schoolteacher, died when he was six years old. When he was about eight years old, his mother remarried and he spent the next eight years on his uncle's farm, just outside the village of Owego, New York, remembering the little learning his father had bequeathed him, getting what more he could out of three or four winter terms in the district school, terms that never lasted longer than four months. But for children in the right sort of homes and communities there are other sources of education than formal schools, and his was of the right sort. There was the Sunday-school library, which, ridicule it as has been our custom for many years now, offered thoughtful minds very real materials of culture and knowledge. His uncle made large use of the Sunday-school library in Owego, reading aloud to the family from the books which made solid contribution to intellectual development. There was also the New York *Observer,* which, with the New York *Tribune,* kept the boy's world informed of ecumenical events and ideas. There were spelling matches, and once, as he recalled in his *Recollections,* there was a debate, which he won, a debate that grew out of the great discussions in Congress from the '50's on. He studied for weeks preceding the debate, securing the speeches of Seward and Wade and Hale and Giddings and others, and beginning that vigorous interest in public affairs which characterized his ministry and, to a remarkable degree, shaped his career.

What took him into the Christian ministry, as far as human circumstances are to be assigned, must be found in the religious life and experiences of his boyhood and youth. It was out of his own religious quest and the misunderstandings through which he pursued it, that his liberal faith ultimately rose, to be given a philosophy by Horace Bushnell and a framework by the social movement of the time. In his early life and the community in which he lived, going to church was as regular as going to dinner, and while the decade and a half from 1836 to 1851 was a long time later than the tough-minded Puritanism of three-hour sermons and sixty-minute prayers, churchgoing in Owego was no Happy-half-hour-with-the Almighty. There was the morning service with preaching; then an intermission of an hour and a half, an intermission filled by the Sunday-school session; then another preaching service. Preaching for the most part meant theological sermons which, whatever they did for the mind, were trials to the flesh; though once in awhile some younger man would strike a fresh and attractive note and give religion a transient aspect of reality. One of the preachers, of some note at the time, whom he frequently heard was a popular evangelist named Jacob Knapp, one of whose pulpit *tours de force* was a description, in very vivid terms, of hell as a pit of roaring flames out of which up the sides of the pit sinners were forever trying to crawl while devils with pitchforks flung them back.

The Millerite excitement swept over the community in his seventh year, with its expectation of the end of the world in 1843. The approaching cataclysm cast an appropriate shadow over the boy's mind, but the shadow lifted when, after the failure of the Millerite schedule, the holocaust was postponed until 1860. With that many years ahead of him he decided that he did not need to worry yet. Amid these and other influences playing on the sensitive spirit of a child, he searched for his own religious faith and certainty, and there are few passages of modern biography more revealing than that in which Doctor Gladden described his boyhood quest:

I cannot lay my hand on my heart and say that the churchgoing helped me to solve my religious problems. In fact, it made those problems more and more tangled and troublesome. I wanted to find my way into the peace of God, into the assurance of his friendship, and that I could not do. I understood that I, with all the rest of mankind, had "by the fall lost communion with God and was under his wrath and curse, and so made liable to all the miseries of this life, to death itself and the pains of hell forever." Of the exact truth of this statement I had not the shadow of doubt. But I understood that there was a way by which I could escape from this curse and regain this lost communion. . . . I would gladly have exchanged for it not only every sinful pleasure, but all the pleasures that were not sinful. It will hardly be credited today, but I felt that being a Christian would mean, for me, giving up all my boyish sports—ballplaying, coasting, fishing; and I was more than ready to make that sacrifice. So I kept trying, for years, to gain that assurance of the favor of God of which I heard people talking, and which, I felt sure, some of them must possess. I listened, in prayer meeting and revival meeting, to what they said about it; I noted with the greatest care the steps that must be taken, and I tried to do just what I was told to do. I was to "give myself away," in a serious and complete self-dedication. I suppose that I shall be far within the truth if I say that I tried to do that, a thousand times. But I understood that when I had done it, properly, I should have an immediate knowledge of the fact that it had been properly done; some evidence in my consciousness that could not be mistaken; that a light would break in, or a burden roll off, or that some other emotional or ecstatic experience would supervene; and when nothing of the kind occurred, the inevitable conclusion was that my effort had been fruitless; that I had failed to commend myself to the favor of God, and was still under his wrath and curse. It is not a good thing for any well-meaning soul to be left in that predicament. To feel that, in spite of your best endeavors, you are an alien and an outcast from the family of God is not encouraging to virtue; it tends to carelessness and irreverence. I have often wondered, in later years, that my faith did not give way; that I did not become an atheist. It was the memory of my father, and the consistent piety of my uncle, I suppose, which made that impossible. But that little unplastered room under the rafters in the old farmhouse, where I lay so many nights, when the house was still, looking out through the casement upon the unpitying stars, has a story to tell of a soul in great perplexity and trouble because it could not find God.[2]

He was seventeen when his uncle decided that his aptitudes were not for agriculture, and there is no record in his *Recollections* that the decision brought him any grief. Where his uncle thought the boy's talents lay is seen in the fact that he secured for him a four years' apprenticeship with the Democratic newspaper of Owego. The terms of the apprenticeship included his board in the home of the editor, a little room with a single window under the eaves, his laundry and cash compensation in the amounts of thirty, forty, sixty and one hundred dollars annually.

In the early fifties such a change from a farm to a town of five thousand or more could not but be epochal in a boy's life; and Owego was not without some superior advantages. It offered the ap-

[2]*Recollections,* pp. 34ff.

prentice, with his residence in the editor's home and his contacts with the events of the community, social outlooks not usually present in small towns. A family by the name of Thompson, well known at the time, occupied a place in its life, for its members had something of fame in art. N. P. Willis lived there also, and there wrote his *Letters From Under a Bridge;* and before the printer's apprentice had gone away to college a campaign Glee Club was being led by a young man whose residence in Owego was to give it later its only claim to renown, his name being Thomas C. Platt.

These years of Gladden's apprenticeship, together with his academy life in Owego which immediately followed, were great years in American history. They were the time of the Fugitive Slave law, of the growth of Abolition sentiments, of the approaching storm of Civil War. Only a couple of years before he began his apprenticeship the young Presbyterian minister of Owego had prayed in public that "we might remember our brethren in bonds, as bound with them," and had been dismissed from his pulpit by an indignant majority of his congregation. *Uncle Tom's Cabin* was marching through the North, and Stephen A. Douglas, at the height of his career, was securing the repeal of the Missouri Compromise. The eloquence of Neal Dow was creating a Prohibition party, unorganized as yet but effective, and the Good Templars were multiplying in numbers and influence. Altogether it was a young man's decade, and this particular young man was alive to all the stir and enterprise of politics and propaganda. If we knew nothing of what his lifework afterward became, we should know that in any case it would be colored and shaped by the social interests, the sympathies, and sense of responsibility acquired even before he went to college.

The churches were feeling and, for the most part, participating in the ferment of the times. The Presbyterian and Episcopal Churches were somewhat slow to respond to the new concern for humanitarianism, holding rather firmly to the theological and sacramentarian interpretations of religion; but the others reacted promptly and took their part quickly in the ethical strife of the period. The young Presbyterian minister who had lost his Owego pulpit because of his prayer for the slaves was brought back to the town to become the minister of a Congregational church formed by the Presbyterians who had seceded after his dismissal. Young Washington Gladden knew him and came at this time to know the direction his own religion if not his lifework must take. "It was not an individualistic pietism that appealed to me; it was a religion that laid hold upon life with both hands, and proposed, first and foremost, to realize the kingdom of God in this world."[3]

In September, 1856, he entered Williams College, graduating in June, 1859. Mark Hopkins

[3] Gladden: *Recollections,* p. 63.

was president of the institution and in 1856 was in his prime; his brother Albert was a member of the faculty, with a more positive and profound religious influence upon the student life than any of his colleagues. John Bascom, afterward president of the University of Wisconsin, was professor of rhetoric, and to him Gladden declared himself under greatest obligations of gratitude. Of his student contemporaries he mentions only a few, Henry M. Alden and Horace E. Scudder, afterward editors of *Harper's Monthly* and *The Atlantic,* being among them. He made friends with Samuel Bowles and Josiah G. Holland, who were editors of the Springfield *Republican.* He was interested in the college music. He did his work in the classroom. But one suspects that he was more interested in what was transpiring beyond the campus during those three pregnant years. Around the world dramatic and terrible events marked their progress. In India the Sepoy Rebellion flamed out in atrocities and terror; in Europe the Treaty of Paris ended the Crimean War; in the Orient Japan was opened to foreigners and the opium war was forced upon China. In this country it was the time of Bleeding Kansas, with John Brown's massacre at Potawattomie a few weeks before Gladden entered college and his capture of Harper's Ferry and his execution at Charles Town, a few months after Gladden had graduated. It was the time during which Lawrence was sacked and burned, the Dred Scott decision declared that Negroes had no constitutional rights, and Lincoln and Douglas conducted the immemorial debates that culminated as far as Douglas was concerned in the Freeport Heresy.

After his graduation Gladden returned to Owego and, like Horace Bushnell, began his public career by teaching, becoming principal of the Owego school. In his boardinghouse he formed a friendship with a young preacher recently settled in Owego as the minister of the Congregational Church, Moses Coit Tyler, and under his direction the schoolteacher began seriously to study theology. He was licensed to preach by the local Association of Congregational Churches, the Rev. Thomas K. Beecher, of Elmira, being the moderator. It was expected, Doctor Gladden recollected later, that he would exercise his gifts in schoolhouses and country churches as infrequent occasion offered; and it was this which he did for sometime until, in 1860, led by opportunity and misled by ignorance into an impossible situation, he became minister of a curious Brooklyn congregation, born in ecclesiastical sin if not conceived in iniquity, which had been formed by secessionists from a Methodist Episcopal church who had quarreled over a preacher. It called itself the First Congregational Methodist Church.

A biography cannot be compressed into a single chapter, certainly not the biography of a man whose career began amid the whirlwind controversies of the Civil War. The war itself and his experiences as a young preacher during the conflict, its effect upon his mind, are taken for granted without further reference except that, although he was only twenty-five years old when it began, he took no part in it until, late in 1863, he learned from a half brother that his only brother had been wounded and was reported as missing after an engagement. Then he secured an appointment with the Christian Commission and went to the front to find his brother, serving with the Commission until in the interest of his health, in June, 1864, he returned to even more peaceful pursuits. In 1865 he entered upon a pastorate in North Adams, Massachusetts, which was to continue for five years, during which Horace Bushnell, whose volume *God in Christ* had given him his theology, became a personal friend.

In 1871 he became editor of the New York *Independent,* resigning, four years later, because of differences between himself and the business management over a question of professional ethics. These four years made their contribution to his future usefulness as they disciplined his expression to the simple, direct style that characterizes his informing books. They fostered his vivid interest in all civic and social as well as religious concerns, and helped in the development of his practical common sense in judging and reacting toward social challenges. They were not uninteresting years from the viewpoint of journalism. They were the years during which Horace Greeley ran for the Presidency against General Grant; the Tweed ring was destroyed and "Boss" Tweed sentenced to the penitentiary; the scandal of the

Union Pacific Railroad and the American Credit Mobilier broke, revealing the fact that members of Congress and senators had been sold railway stock at par value when it was selling on the open market at twice par value while those "on the inside," when the situation was ripe, received $3,500 for every $1,000 invested. The Vice-President, Senator Patterson of New Jersey, and James A. Garfield, later to be President, were among those implicated. It was during these four years also that William Worth Belknap, Grant's secretary of war, and Mrs. Belknap were charged with accepting money in connection with the disposal of public offices and Belknap's resignation was received as a confession of his guilt. It was in 1884, Gladden's last year as editor, that out in Chicago David Swing was tried for heresy and acquitted. About none of these great and dramatic interests could Washington Gladden have been unconcerned, on none of them could he have been silent; and when at the close of his editorship he entered upon the pastorate of a church in Springfield, Massachusetts, he was not only returning to New England and its habits of mind, he was returning with immeasurably broadened sympathies and with greatly enlarged conceptions of pastoral and pulpit responsibility.

If Gladden's liberal faith and liberalizing influence can scarcely be associated with the New-England theology even as a protest, seeing that his only direct theological connection with New England was through Bushnell's "heresy," there is a curious fitness in his being a minister of Springfield's Congregationalism. For Springfield had been founded two hundred thirty-nine years before Gladden's arrival by a certain William Pyncheon, whose name takes one back at once to *The House of the Seven Gables*, and not thence only, but to a book which he himself had written and had published in England, entitled *The Meritorious Price of Our Redemption*. In England it raised such a volume of Puritan criticism that the Great and General Court of Boston saw to it that when the ship arrived on which the books were being brought to America, they were practically all seized and burned, although, of course, a few escaped. The work itself was fearfully Calvinistic, but it denied that Christ actually suffered the pains of hell, including remorse; so the public hangman burned the imported copies on Boston Common, and in 1652 William Pyncheon, tired of the criticism and constant censure, went back to England and disappeared from history, leaving his children in Puritan Massachusetts; and two hundred and twenty-three years later Washington Gladden, whose liberal beliefs would have shocked him beyond measure, began his ministry among the Pyncheon descendants.

Eight years later, December, 1882, he enters his ministry in Columbus, Ohio, and at once he begins an almost nationwide service. The experience and study of a quarter of a century; the sympathies broadened by the vivid epoch through which already he had lived; the insights born of innumerable personal contacts and the disciplines of the editorship; the effect of New England and of New York City—all wrought their consummation in a usefulness which places him among the most eminent and influential men of his time, and made him certainly the most eminent and influential exponent in the American pulpit of what we now call the social gospel. Those who do not know something of the man and his work from that December date until his death are ignorant of one of the great figures of twentieth-century Protestantism.

In his *Recollections* he has a chapter entitled "A Widening Vocation" which is an inevitable description, not alone of the contents of that particular chapter, but of his life itself, especially of his ministry of thirty some years in and from Columbus. In New England he had taken part in the liberalizing of Congregational theology, particularly in respect of what became known as the doctrine of Second Probation; and in Columbus he was to continue his contribution to theological liberalism and, in addition, take high place in the growing movement which from one point of view sought to socialize Christianity and, from another point of view, aimed at Christianizing social, political, and industrial relationships.

Hardly anything less than a volume would suffice adequately to portray his vocation as it widened down these years, or indicate the sometimes astonishing influence which he exercised in areas of social experience hitherto unassociated with the preaching ministry. What can be done within the limits of this chapter will be, at best, but a hurried summary from which many significant enterprises and achievements will, of necessity, be omitted. Labor disturbances, strikes in several places and industries, particularly a conflict between the operators and coal miners in the Hocking Valley in 1884, brought him face to face at short distance with the challenge of the responsibility of the Church in modern industry. He delivered a series of addresses on Sunday evenings in his Columbus pulpit, dealing with the subject. It is a pulpit technic familiar enough now, but very new and, to the majority of Christians, very questionable then. Most of these addresses, some time later, were printed in *The Century Magazine*. In 1886, during a violent strike in Cleveland, the efforts of a public-minded and philanthropic citizen brought together a great meeting of employers and striking employees in the Music Hall, to which Doctor Gladden had been invited to speak. He found himself facing an audience, not only large but critical, with some members of it hostile. But as he spoke on "Is It War Or Peace?" criticism and hostility gave way to searching judgment and the beginnings of a new mutual understanding. A week later, by request, he gave the same address to a large gathering of business and professional men in Boston which had been assembled in an unusually significant meeting. The governor of Massachusetts presided and with him on the platform were eminent and representative leaders of the commonwealth. A few days later he was again in Boston delivering that same address to another audience, composed largely of workingmen, with labor leaders on the platform. This address, together with those which he had delivered a couple of years earlier in his pulpit, was published in a volume that created and popularized a phrase and established his reputation; it was the volume, widely read at the time, entitled *Applied Christianity.*

It is illustrative of the range of his interests and the plain, practical, and successful realism of the man to recall the change of election laws in Ohio with which he is identified. Ohio elected its state officers in October, so that in the years of a Presidential election in November, the public saw business interrupted, the interests of the citizens distracted, and taxpayers saddled with the additional and unnecessary expense involved in two campaigns and elections. It was Doctor Gladden, not a businessman nor a legislator, who began an agitation for a change in the election laws, an agitation which, without a public meeting, a speech, or a committee, resulted in an amendment that moved the state election into November.

His contacts with the state university acquainted him quite naturally with the increasing perplexity of students concerning the Bible, the confusion created in their minds in respect of such subjects as Inspiration, Authority, Infallibility, and the revolutionary changes in attitudes toward the

Bible wrought by historical criticism and modern science. With them in mind he preached a series of sermons on "Who Wrote the Bible?" afterward published in a small volume with the same title. For years it was a manual in Bible-study classes, Y. M. C. A. groups, and the like. Today it reads like a very Victorian and conservative treatise, but it was on the firing line of progressive religion thirty-five years ago.

Sermons in his pulpit and lectures at Yale, Cornell, Mansfield College, Oxford, Meadville Theological Seminary, Grinnel College, Harvard, Drew Theological Seminary, and elsewhere, resulted in volumes on *Burning Questions, Tools and the Man, Property and Industry Under Christian Law, Witnesses of The Light, Social Salvation, Christianity and Socialism*, the titles of which indicate their character, and the direction of his ministry. His total literary product, as published, numbers thirty-two volumes, large and small, all of them timely and some of them of still creative and corrective value.

He was attracted to the subjects of municipal government and the omnipresent problems presented by its inefficiency. Forty years ago the development of clubs and civic and cultural associations had hardly more than begun; at least it had gone but a little way in comparison with the multiplicity of organizations today; so that his approach to the creation of good municipal government was far more fresh and stimulating than it would be at this time. He wrote a story, "The

Cosmopolis City Club," published as a serial in *The Century Magazine* and republished in a small book in 1893. A direct result of the story was an almost immediate increase in the number of municipal clubs, many of them patterned upon the "Cosmopolis Club." He was invited, also, to participate in the organization of the City Club of New York; and the formation of the Chicago Civic Federation was ascribed to the influence of his story.

His concern with municipal affairs, however, was not merely that of a spectator and critic. When it became known that members of the Columbus City Council had entered upon a conspiracy of graft and that the forthcoming elections to the Council were being promoted in the interest of the conspiracy, Doctor Gladden announced himself as a candidate from his ward. His position in the city was so assured and his character so commanding that without a canvass on his part, without a single address, and practically without his mentioning the matter in private conversation, he was elected. He served his term of two years, not nominally, but actually giving himself thoroughly to the demands of the office during a period in which very serious municipal enterprises and policies were conducted.

It has already been intimated, even in so brief a sketch of a remarkably active and "widening vocation," that his interests and influence were by no means local. A final incident may stand as illustrative of this aspect of his life. In 1902 the editor of the Cincinnati *Post* was one of the public-minded citizens throughout the country who desired President Roosevelt's intervention in the struggle between the anthracite coal operators and miners in Pennsylvania. He came to Columbus to confer with Doctor Gladden concerning an approach to the President, specifically concerning a petition which he thought might be circulated advantageously. It was Doctor Gladden who wrote the petition which was widely circulated and signed by thousands of people and afterward sent to President Roosevelt asking him to intervene; and this petition, in numerous copies, was among the more powerful of the influences which led the President to his unprecedented but very wise action.

The emphasis in this chapter seems to be on Gladden's activity rather than on his theology. It is the emphasis which, doubtless, most nearly corresponds to his own evaluation. Yet his activity was the expression of a theology of which he was both conscious and certain. A body of belief which he could say he derived from Horace Bushnell would be no nearer the New-England Calvinism, in which he had been raised, than Bushnell's own theology. "The God of Cotton Mather or Edward Payson," Gladden wrote, "could hardly have lived in the same heaven with the God of Dwight Moody or Phillips Brooks," and Gladden could not have lived with him anywhere. "The whole grim, ghastly, appalling fabrication," is the way in which he describes Calvinism, in one of his paragraphs. Christianity he discusses in one of his most revealing chapters as rising from three sources: the World of Nature; Humanity, coming to its sublime consummation in the historic Jesus; and "that divine Spirit who is always in the world, and always waiting upon the threshold of every man's thought, and in the subconscious depths of every man's feeling, to enlighten our understanding and purify our desires."[4] Nature, humanity, and the divine spirit on the threshold of every man's thought, remind one of the shallow skepticism of the author of *Robert Elsmere,* that the ordinary human life and experience slowly evolving through history is the real source of religion, to be realized if one will but listen to the voice of the Eternal Friend speaking in his own soul through conscience and society and nature. But Gladden, who died before the words just quoted were written, did not fall into the rather stupid inconsistency of Mrs. Ward. If all we have is the Voice speaking through Conscience, Society, and Nature, not even a novelist could be sure it was the voice of a friend, let alone an Eternal Friend. Gladden saves the consistency as well as the orthodoxy of his utterance when he writes "who" of the Divine Spirit. At the atonement, his break with evangelical as well as Calvinistic orthodoxy is fairly complete when he can write of "that propitiation in conscience which is the atoning work of Christ."[5] He was no Calvinist but he was a Trinitarian, and if the language

[4] *The Church and Modern Life,* p. 26.
[5] Gladden: *How Much Is Left of the Old Doctrines?* p. 193.

with which he expresses his conception of the nature of Jesus could hardly have satisfied the theologians of his generation, no one can doubt the object or strength of his loyalty.

> The manifestation of the life of God in Jesus Christ we call The Incarnation; and it was a manifestation so much more perfect than any other that the world has seen that we do well to put the definite article before the word. Yet it is a mistake to overlook the fact that God dwells in every good man, and manifests himself through him, and whenever in any character, the great qualities of truth and justice and purity and courage and honor and kindness are exhibited, we see some reflection of the character of God.[6]

In the midst of his activities—and no preacher ever lived a busier life—he was forthright in his denial of Calvinism and in his own career illustrated the motivating power of truly liberal and Christian convictions.

> The whole grim, ghastly, appalling fabrication is built upon a deification of will. The central element of personality, men said, is the will. God's will must then be the foundation of theology; take the principle of will, make it omnipotent and absolute, subordinate to it every other element of character, then deduce your theology from the principle, and you will have the Augustinian Calvinism.[7]

It is a very far cry from Cotton Mather to Washington Gladden. In the Puritan Commonwealth the magistrates were practically servants of the

[6] *The Church and Modern Life,* p. 24f.
[7] Gladden: *How Much Is Left of the Old Doctrines?* p. 213.

Church, and the Church's social and political attitudes were those held by the clergy. In twentieth-century America the Church has little apparent influence on government, and its decisive attitudes are those of the laity, who are by no means always in agreement with the clergy. The distance between such a conduct of Christianity and that of Washington Gladden cannot be registered by the calendar. But there is a real continuity in which they both participate; a continuity of Christian purpose to establish amid the strifes and passions of men, amid the shadows and conflicts of the temporal world, the unmistakable kingdom of God. The extreme divergence between the seventeenth and twentieth centuries, of which Cotton Mather and Gladden are spokesmen, is a divergence in method and instruments. Cotton Mather administered civil affairs as a department of the Church in the interests of theology. Gladden sought to permeate civil affairs as a field for religion in the interests of human life. The aim of Christianity, he said, is a perfect man in a perfect society, and he staked his life on the truth that Christianity has to be equally concerned with each. Mather dominated social relations with a creed looking always toward another world. Gladden informed and directed social relations with an ethic that pursued justice in this world. Mather attempted a theocracy under the rigid control of the Church; Gladden was committed to a democracy conducted in the spirit of Jesus. No man more thoroughly illustrates the truth, too easily obscured by contemporary controversies, that the progress of pulpit liberalism has been a return to the Gospels.

References

Adams and Vannest, *The Record of America.*

Addams, Jane, *Twenty Years at Hull House.*

Bennett, John C., *Social Salvation.*

Dewey, John, *Liberalism in Social Action.*

Douglass and Brunner, *The Protestant Church as a Social Institution.*

Gauss, Christian, *A Primer for Tomorrow.*

Gladden, Washington, *Recollections.*

Gladden, Washington, *The Church and Modern Life.*

Morrison, Charles C., *The Social Gospel and the Christian Cultus.*

Niebuhr, Pauck and Miller, *The Church Against the World.*

Rauschenbusch, Walter, *A Theology for the Social Gospel.*

Wallace, Henry A., *Statesmanship and Religion.*

X

WHAT OF THE LIGHT?

X

WHAT OF THE LIGHT?

AND now what does a study of such preachers as these, what would a study of all the significant preachers of two hundred and fifty years of American history have to teach us? This: on the very surface, that religion has been, if not the deepest, surely one of the constant and most powerful forces in the making of our American history and life. It impelled and sustained the adventure of the Puritans. It undergirded and guided all of the major colonial settlements except perhaps New York and Virginia. It re-enforced where it did not inspire the spirit of independence which issued in the Revolution and the Republic. It played around the formative generations and expanding movements of the nation in the Great Awakening under Jonathan Edwards and George Whitefield, and was the very mother of American democracy. It gave color and direction, though the volume does not touch upon the subject, to the most characteristic American literature, in the Concord School, of which Hawthorne was the representative; and it was an inescapable and determining influence, in the sixties, in the march of emancipation and, through Henry Ward Beecher, Peter Cartwright, and a host of less famous preachers, the cause of the North. This pervasiveness of religion in the enterprises of common life is a disclosure made at every stage of our history. A modern witness speaks from an unexpected quarter.

> A review of the entire evidence indicates that institutional religion is characterized by a high degree of stability and persistence. During the period, the Church has held fast to its historic moorings, and has retained the allegiance, in form at least, of half the population.[1]

That, in turn, suggests to those accustomed to look beneath surface moods, that no movements in present-day society, no developing national policies—those against war, for industrial reform, for domestic reconstruction of any kind—can promise permanence or guarantee moral insights if they are disassociated from the convictions which only religious loyalties and ideals can sustain. "No great civilization has ever outlasted the demise of its religious faith."[2]

This is not merely a passing remark. There are benevolent and serious minds today which, making enthusiasm for humanity a substitute for personal religion, have given the spacious name of humanism a shrunken significance. Loyalty to human society is their one devotion. Their hope of new worlds is in the future of modern science. For

[1] From *Recent Social Trends in the United States.*

[2] Leighton: *Religion and the Mind of Today,* p. 51.

them the true pattern of human life is not a society subject to a divine Lord, but the normal process of development obtaining in the growth of a child to maturity. Biology, not political science, furnishes their analogy of human life. Divine revelation, distinctive Scriptures, the mysterious but experienced means of grace, the spiritual values hitherto found in the great Christian tradition, are considered fictions, or at least irrelevant; a conception which, practically applied, reaches its most consistent practice and consummation in the country and people of Liu Yutang. "A characteristic of all Chinese novels," he writes in what has been called the most perceptive book ever written on the Chinese, "A characteristic of all Chinese novels is the incessant and never tiring enumeration of the names of dishes served at a family feast or a traveler's supper in an inn, followed frequently by stomach aches and trips to the vacant lot which is the natural man's toilet. So the Chinese novelists write, and so the Chinese men and women live, and it is a life too full to be occupied with thoughts of immortality."[3] What the humanists seem to forget is that fullness of life means nothing if it is concerned only with quantity. An existence so full of food and physical reactions, or even of social enthusiasms, that it has no time to be occupied with any concerns other than physical or even social experiences; life so full of biology that it has no time to be con-

[3] Liu Yutang: *My Country and My People,* p. 104.

cerned with what Doctor Cadman has called "those emotions and meditations which are the reverberations of eternity within the human spirit," can have little permanent attraction for men and women who desire to do more than exist. Human experience still confirms Carlyle's dictum that "We cannot stand firm in time until we have gained a foothold somewhere beyond time."

Stuart Sherman characterized this humanistic movement as seeking "not primarily to reclaim man for God but to reclaim him for civil society; not so much to fit him with wings as to persuade him to shed the horns and hoofs which he has been wearing in his long *aprè-midi d'un faune*."[4] The aim has considerable to commend it, but there are grave disadvantages which a French phrase cannot wholly hide. One must know what kind of society it is for which man is to be fitted, and the kind that ignores what religion counts most important does not require much reclaiming nor impose much difficulty in the fitting process. On the other hand it raises fears. If man's long afternoon-of-a-faun is to be followed, as it will be if there is no one here but man, by the twilight of a faun, or by a faun's morning, man would better keep his hoofs and horns; he may need them.

Intelligent men, of course, will not be blind to the challenge of contemporary humanism. "The worth of religion and of faith must be discovered

[4] *On Contemporary Literature,* p. 13.

and vindicated here and now."[5] They may well emulate its bold acceptance of responsibility for social conditions and their perfectibility. But humanism has nothing in itself to warrant confidence that anything satisfactory will come of its responsibility, and history is against its program. As Professor Douglas C. Macintosh has said, literary humanism builds on the distinctively human, but this present-day religious humanism builds on the merely human; and to the challenge of either history replies that men who build their life and social conduct upon only an enthusiasm for humanity cannot long retain the enthusiasm. The selfish individual fails of satisfaction, as we know; but it has not always been recognized that the selfish society fails in the same way. The servants of society who, across two thousand years, have grandly wrought for this world have been for the most part tremendously concerned for another world. "A humanist is a man who is on the way from something to something."[6] But while men who are simply traveling may be good companions, they are likely to be poor guides; for what most concerns serious travelers is their destination. If God is our dwelling place, as the psalmist phrased it, we can be enthusiastic for the welfare of the whole family. But men have found it impossible to consider one another as brothers

[5] Nixon: *An Emerging Faith,* p. 33.

[6] Bernard Iddings Bell: *Unfashionable Convictions,* p. 9.

if they lose sight of the fact that God is their Father.

On the other hand, there is today a definite and pervasive revival of Calvinism of a kind. Karl Barth, a preacher who found himself, like many less famous preachers, unhappily without material to preach, may be said to have begun this revival; but the urgency for it was vibrant in the collapsed idealism and disappointed hopes which followed the Armistice. Barth could see no way out of the human tragedy but he could describe it as one hundred per cent terrible and then, like Gabriel in *The Green Pastures,* call God to pass a miracle of redemption, without trying to find any sense in the confusion his technic illustrates. As Henry Nelson Wieman has said:

> Barth brought forth his theology, not to solve any problems and not to give any direction to human life, not even to quicken aspiration and outreach, but to provide drama for preaching. Paint the heavens black, then show a glorious gleam that does not illumine anything nor lead anywhere but gives a tremendous shiver and dazzle. That makes a wonderful sermon. That is the theology of Karl Barth. It will not last, but it may sweep the world. It is for religion what the Dada movement was for art. It meets a similar need and may have a similar career. Dada today is dead.

Such a characterization of Barthianism doubtless contradicts the judgments and disturbs the feelings of those religious circles in which affirmation is made to do duty for understanding. But Barth and his followers land precisely where the older and more intelligent as well as intelligible Calvinism landed—in hopeless inconsistency in the face of life. Having declared the uselessness of any attempt to discriminate truth from falsehood, he speedily makes other assertions about God and the way of salvation which, he assures us, are revealed to him by the Holy Spirit. He eats his theological cake and claims he still has it in his hand by adopting a modern, scientific view of Scriptures and then using them as if they were the most literal, automatic, inerrant, and only revelation of the will and ways of God. He out-Carlyles Carlyle in believing that God was in the past and will be in the future but is wholly out of the present. Groping, hopeless humanity is therefore forever confronted with a moral obligation it never could or can fulfill. It must be saved by a God from whom it is forever banished, and in the face of desperate social and pagan ethics and a naturalism which trends toward the baser modes of life, which history and the gospel call it to transform, must admit its helplessness and take refuge in cryptic conceptions of the awful, remote yet imminent sovereignty of an Almighty as far from Jesus' conception of God as can well be imagined outside of heathenism or Homer. Reading, amid much that is wise and spiritually provocative in Barth's discourses, the emotional outbursts of curious paradox which in other forms of utterance would be called bombast, one recalls Eugene Bagger's penetrating comment on Francis Joseph that "He went on repeating his own formulas until he came to believe that he was listening to the voice of history."[7] Only, to Barth his own formulas seem to have become the voice of God, which, according to himself, no one can hear. So good men are betrayed by their earnestness into a religion of escape; repudiating the idea of escaping, while they fling all responsibility on a God whom they cannot reach and around whose possible reaching them there is flung such a mist and furore of words that the boldest can have little hope. Meanwhile the world waits for the application of the mind of a Galilean who was neither cryptic nor explosive and who found God so near to humanity that He was forced to say to His immediate and rather commonplace friends, "Ye are the salt of the earth. Let your light shine."

There is another mode in which this contemporary flight from history takes expression. It is the insinuation of Predestination and Necessity in an emotional assumption of human freedom; an affirmation of Calvinism in the language of Arminian apology, the most effective illustration of this being Professor Edwin Lewis's *A Christian Manifesto*. There are utterances in this notable volume to re-enforce the faith of liberal minds. There is in it a constant, if not always consistent, note of responsibility greatly needed today. As Bishop Francis J. McConnell wrote of it, even if modernists do not accept it, it has to be reckoned with.

[7] Bagger: *Francis Joseph,* p. 25.

It is not only an ungrateful business, it is difficult to criticize *A Christian Manifesto* with any satisfaction because, though one may disagree with it very positively, at the same time he will feel the note of a genuine endeavor for sincerity, a genuine evangelical passion for the evangelical result. Professor Lewis's place among contemporary theologians is as sure as the esteem in which his Christian piety is held by those privileged to know him, and it is no contradiction of the approval which the reading public has given to the volume to ask whether or not his vigorous and kindling religious assurance has led him into a Barthian Calvinism which is no less unfortunate for being the product of his own radiant experience and prophetic earnestness.

In the chapter on "The Foredoomed Man" there is an eloquent paragraph descriptive of the God for whom Christianity calls; who has power to do new things and is larger than any part of the instrumentality through which He works; who can speak to men and who has the right to use men as He pleases; who is able to do things to Himself and who "even wounds himself, crucifies himself, slays himself." Doctor Lewis piles up tribute upon tribute to the omnipotent God, whose truest symbol is "a Man on a Cross." The cumulative effect is unmistakable, and it would be a mind insensitive to spiritual passion and the insatiable quest of the soul for certainty who did not respond to it; but it is difficult to believe that if God "wounds himself, crucifies himself, slays himself," the "Man on the

Cross" is only a symbol. A symbol must point to a reality greater than itself; and a God "self-slain on his own strange altar," to give a line of Swinburne's a theological cast, raises the question whether there must not be another God somewhere being symbolized, if the slain God is a symbol. The magnificent mystery of the incarnation may be felt, but cannot be reduced to precise statement; it must always bring a luminous cloud to the mount of revelation; but theologians must not give us the sensuous figures of imaginative piety as statements of definable faith. Gilbert Chesterton long since wrote about God being forsaken by God, but metaphors, however stirring, will not do in theology. The heart makes the theologian, and truth may come in on a tide of feeling; but the language of theology should lessen the confusion which has done much to lead a large portion of the modern mind to regard the doctrine of atonement as irrelevant to life. When one reflects upon Doctor Lewis's noble and moving prose, by which he has been, for the time, carried away, he is likely to discover that the human history of the crucifixion is more bewildering than ever.

There is today an interesting rally of liberal minds to the banner of Divine Absolutism. Dictatorship, not content with its successes along the Mediterranean and in Prussia, is pushing past its conquests in political science, to occupy the literature of American Protestantism. But there, as elsewhere, serious account must be taken of its implications. A robust Arminian becomes skeptical of a God as unconditioned in His relations with His own creatures as *A Christian Manifesto* seems to suggest. If an omnipotent God has a right to use men in His own way and for His own purposes, has He not been so using them and thus has produced the actual conditions of human history; or if not, has He not failed to exercise His right, with a wrecked world as a result? In either case is He not responsible for what has happened? If, for the inevitable results of a sinful nature which they have no possibility of avoiding, men are to be penalized by the God who is responsible for their having that sinful nature—and that is the situation with a God who has the unconditioned right to use men in His own way—then it is hard to answer the skeptical charge that there is something wrong with His moral character. On the other hand, if the fundamental disharmony at the very center of original human nature, from which specific sinful acts are an inevitable issue, is an inheritance which we do not ourselves choose, and an unconditioned God can rescue us from the consequences in which we are involved by the original estate in which He fixed us, only by slaying Himself, the Great Deed witnesses His compassion, but does it not discredit His original intelligence?

The values for which Doctor Lewis so valiantly contends must be conserved and re-emphasized; but the history of Christian thought, in its ethical expression, warns us away from any theology which even unconsciously seems to invite morally disappointed men to take refuge from their own obligations in an omnipotence responsible at once for their evil nature, and for the good world which that nature may delay but cannot defeat.

Volumes such as Doctor Hugh Thomson Kerr's *A God-Centered Faith,* display the same unacknowledged and doubtless unintentional tendency to take refuge from responsibility in an arbitrary omnipotence. Ours is a badly managed social order, world-wide in the scope of its wickedness and folly, and our future threatens to be too much for what moral resources men have lately displayed. Accordingly, it is rather difficult not to shuffle the whole sorry business onto the shoulders of the Almighty. But this contemporary literature, as a whole, is likely to disappoint a reader who is disturbed by appearances of inconsistency. One reads an argument for the faith of the Calvinistic Reformers, and then discovers a synthesis of the essentials of the Protestant belief which ignores the distinctive features of Calvinistic theology, but calls the entire achievement Calvinism.

Referring to the gospel preaching and the simple domestic pieties of prayer and hymns in Christian homes before the Reformation, Doctor Kerr, for instance, cites a paragraph of Professor Lindsay to the effect that there was a simple evangelical faith among religious Christians in medieval times, and that it was their thoughts and language which the Reformers wove into the Reformation creeds and developed into the Reformation theology.

But what this really makes clear is that vital

Christian piety has always been fed from the great stream of the gospel running deep beneath the differentiating theologies by which men have divided themselves into opposing communities of faith. To declare that the divine sovereignty was revealed to the reformers is to forget that the entire material of Calvinism lay, as a rich mine, in Saint Augustine, from whom Calvin derived the substance to which he gave expression. Furthermore, if one can totally disregard Augustine and believe that the divine sovereignty was revealed to the Reformers, he could not possibly believe that the interpretation of its details was revealed. Luther and Zwingli and Calvin wove the words and thoughts into Reformation Creeds, but the creeds were quite different from the elements of medieval piety. What was distinctive in the Calvinistic creeds is precisely what the recovery of the gospel, under the influence of liberal preaching, has discarded; and there will be no way out of our contemporary confusion, social or theological, by turning back to genuine Calvinism, or by snatching at the name while offering something from which the Calvinistic substance has been evaporated.

Modern Calvinism declares the fact that God, having provided, in infinite and perfect love, a "way of life and salvation, sufficient for and adapted to the whole lost race of man, doth freely offer this salvation to all men in the gospel." This version would greatly have astonished John Bunyan, writing his personal problem, "That the elect only attained Eternal Life, that I, without scruple, did heartily close withal; but that myself was one of them, there lay the question." And one still hears George A. Gordon's mother rebuke his boyish earnestness: "No; not if predestination is against you. There is no hope."[8] And if anyone, mistaking for original Calvinism the revised modern utterances which merely keep the old labels, objects to so positive a statement, he need only read the life of Jesse Lee to find earnest New-England Calvinists calling the belief that Christ died for all and all might come to salvation, "a damnable doctrine."

One must be grateful for the irenical and gracious spirit of *A God-Centered Faith;* as, indeed, one must be grateful for the historic Presbyterian mind to which the world can never pay its debt. Reject, as men have done, its terrible original theology and its once terrible God, turn away as men please from the new Calvinism which claims the title but has compromised with the rigors of the old Covenanting faith, it remains true that Presbyterianism, more perhaps than any other communion, has evinced, and maintained itself upon what Santayana, in *The Last Puritan,* calls "the inscrutable, invincible preference of the mind for the infinite." But this gratitude ought not to blind one to the fact that while *A God-Centered Faith* would call men back to Calvinism, it apparently ignores the element which was most distinctive and, indeed, descriptive of Calvinism.

[8] Gordon: *My Education and Religion,* p. 69.

And by as much as a modern thesis claims the sanction of an older orthodoxy while proffering something quite different, it inherits the failure of the past and forfeits the advantage which its own merit might claim.

Rejection of even mild Calvinism does not mean that one has to go over to the Unitarian camp, for the two are not as mutually exclusive as has generally been thought. It is by no means just an accident of history that Unitarianism came in revolt against a dominant Calvinism. Channing said that it was not the Trinity which was at first too much for him, it was the lack of freedom. But neither Channing nor his most orthodox Calvinistic opponent recognized the fact that the old predestination-and-election Calvinism which was sure only a few were elected to salvation and the many were elected to be damned, both alike without moral responsibility but wholly for the glory of God, is perilously near being a form of Unitarianism itself. It is Calvin's ruthless utterance that whithersoever we turn our eyes the curse of God meets us, seizing innocent creatures and involving them in our guilt, and he reaches the conclusion that therefore our souls must be overwhelmed with despair. But it would be despair not only of ourselves, but of the character of God. For a God who was all that fierce old Calvinism claimed Him to be, but who did the limited, little, unjust things which Calvinism said He did, would be simply giving the lie to all He is presumed to have testified in revelation as to the character of His Son.

That old Calvinism affirmed the deity of Christ, and then went on in its fearful, Old-Testament fashion to repudiate the divinity of what the Son did. It reversed the testimony of the spectators at the cross, and said through all its bleak business of limited salvation, "He saved himself, others he cannot save."

The one emphasis of Calvinism which must be retained and which the most liberal theology dares not ignore is that of what H. R. MacIntosh called the divine initiative; that, as he put it, God is on the ground first. But beyond that emphasis the modern religious mind, desperately concerned as it is with a way out of or through what a contemporary intellectual, in the note he left before committing suicide, called the mess of life, is not likely to trust for long any attempted return to Calvinism. Because, when it does so, it will come face to face with the fact that necessitarian theology, however tricked out with new phrases and the changing clichès of a phrase-making form of libertary piety, is the denial of morality as well as of personal hope. If Samuel Johnson could ever have gotten Wesley to fold his legs and have their talk out, the two greatest figures of England's eighteenth century would have agreed on Johnson's "I know I am free, and there is an end of it." For Wesley knew that without freedom there is no moral obligation for either one's character or that of the world, and he made a working synthesis of Divine sovereignty and human freedom, which has been acclimated to every period of the liberal tradition. God *is* sovereign; but, unless Jesus is mistaken, His sovereignty is through men rather than in spite of them. Freedom, it is admitted, involves responsibility; but what must be held far more steadfastly than much modern neo-Calvinism indicates, is that responsibility implicates freedom. A good world achieved by predetermining the goodness by omnipotence, no matter what men do or think or desire, would leave them with no more significance in it than a baby on his father's knee with his hands on the steering wheel possesses in driving the car. He enjoys the sensation but has nothing to do with the machine, the road, or the destination. It may be that this is the way the world is managed, but if it is, the *Deus ex Machina* is not the Father of Jesus.

One heartening implication thrusts itself through all this literature of neo-Calvinism, as of frightened liberalism itself, namely, that the great stream of religious reality runs but little changed underneath the shifting theologies by which it is, at different times, described. Longfellow, in his notes to Paradiso, quotes an Italian *Life and Times of Dante*. "Philosophy is the romance of the aged, and Religion the only future history for us all." But in the long run, only those dicta of faith will survive which the total experience of believing men approves. Genuine liberalism in religion is not so much a recovery of the gospel and the Gospels as a record of their expanding truth, as they are continually reread with insights sharpened by fuller scholarship and redeemed by an enlarging ethical consideration from the extravagances of overemphasis which critical and dangerous days from time to time have found necessary in the defense of a beloved community.

Liberalism in theology appears today to be frightened by its own failure in maintaining and expanding the social moralities. It has realized anew the impossibility of social redemption apart from religion and God. But it is in danger of forgetting that while God has redeemed the world, it is men who must save it; and it has mistaken the failure of men for incompetence. But the world is today what it is, not because men have been incompetent but because they have been inconstant. Liberal Protestantism has so far failed to take the objectives set before it by the last advance of a conservatism which came to the end of a day it had served well but could serve no more, because, like Marc Antony, it has been strong enough to conquer the world but not strong enough to resist a temptation. Temptations to compromise with the social and political compulsions of the hour and place have met but half-hearted resistance. The infections of avarice and self-protection which spring from comfortable prosperity; the treason to righteousness so subtly misled by Nationalism; the selfishness which disarms by its masquerade of self-respect; have had their way with men in their social relationships who in personal life have been impeccable of character and heroic in faith. But to conclude that the only way of social regeneration is by a return to an omnipotence which is going to win through in spite of human betrayals, is not only to despair of men, it is to discredit the character of God. A God who succeeds by omnipotence does not need character. All He needs is enough power; and power is not enough to make Him God. Only character can equip the Divine. The only world in which anyone can have confidence, the only world worth living in, is a world in which men's lives are not a reaction to the compulsions of divine power, but are a response to the influences of divine grace. That is the very substance of liberal faith as it is the essential message of the gospel, for it is the practical meaning of the cross.

The increasing purpose reflected in the theological progress reported in these chapters, is the essential ideal of both Cotton Mather's Puritan Commonwealth and the later-day humanists, effectualized in a fashion less mechanical than the Commonwealth, less diffuse and dialectical than humanism. The cross, as the author of *Jesus and the Human Conflict* put it, "is not the end of conflict, but the symbol of the daily struggle."[9] To quote further from a volume which had nothing like the reading public it merited, the "redemptive vocation of the righteous community is the unclaimed legacy of Christianity to-day."[10] Here, perhaps, is the place at which liberal faith needs most to discover itself. One may not be able to avoid a haunting sympathy for the liberal mind

[9] John Dow: *Jesus and the Human Conflict,* p. 284.
[10] *Ibid.,* p. 285.

finding itself shocked and disillusioned by the collapse of idealism which has characterized the past twenty years; but liberalism is not bankrupt, either in theology or politics. It has simply been so concerned with its ideas and the panorama of its world that it has lost sight of its major apostasy. What it needs to recover from the Scripture and Christian history is not the victorious foreordinations of the Almighty, but the productive obligation of the community.

During a recent visit of Toyohiko Kagawa to one of our cities, he addressed perhaps a thousand church members at luncheon in one of the most expensive hotels. As the gathering dispersed afterward, an official in the government asked one of the committeemen prominent in the management of Kagawa's visit, how the Church could be interested in support of the government's attempts to establish consumers' co-operatives as a distinctly social service. He was given the impression that the Church would not be interested in such co-operation. But if the redemptive vocation of the righteous community were an axiom of religious thought, as the prophets understood it, as the liberalizing pulpits have declared it with increasing emphasis, and as Jesus undoubtedly intended it to be, such a reply would have been impossible. It is quite easy to put the liberal faith into generalizations where original orthodoxy was terrifying by its specifications. What is needed, however, is neither the terror of direful specifications nor the complacence of easy generalizations, but the establishment of New Testament theology as the principle governing the practical responsibilities of the social life of men.

Bergson's *The Two Sources of Morality and Religion* glows on page after page with profound thought eloquently phrased. One such page discusses the mystics.

> That which they have allowed to flow into them is a stream flowing down and seeking through them to reach their fellow men; the necessity to spread around them what they have received affects them like an onslaught of love. A love which each one of them stamps with his own personality. A love which is in each of them an entirely new emotion, capable of transposing human life into another tone. A love which thus causes each of them to be loved for himself, so that through him, and for him, other men will open their souls to the love of humanity. A love which can be just as well passed on through the medium of a person who has attached himself to them or to their evergreen memory and formed his life on that pattern.[11]

This is, as far as it goes, very close to an essential Christian interpretation. But the failure of mysticism now is that it does not get outside the mystic, a failure in which modern theology participates. The fatal dualism of modern religion is that the social gospel seems barren of an adequate theology, notwithstanding the work of Walter Rauschenbusch, and theological religion has little if any effective social machinery. Modern

[11]Bergson: *The Two Sources of Morality and Religion,* p. 90.

theology must have tools put into its hands for translating redemption into social consequences, while the tool makers need to do their work in the clear light of theological verities. The focus of the theological and practical energies which must thus be synthesized is Christ. Through Him is the only genuine continuity of religion to day with the religious past, as in Him is the only significant goal of the future. With every generation He has become better known, more significant, more and more the center and circumference of Christianity. Today, amid whatever criticisms may be leveled at contemporary religion, the use of the Bible, the forms of worship, and the conduct of the churches, criticism, though not wholly silent in the presence of Christ, is subdued by the spiritual reality He incarnates. He is real, He is commanding, and it will save us from immense confusion to remember that while He has been the center of divisive arguments and exclusive theologies, He is also the only Figure in the world's history whose judgment on a question of moral principle in nineteen hundred years has not been found to be mistaken.

It was in its apprehension and representation of Christ that the New-England theology failed. It failed to appreciate His character, and quite missed what seems, today, to be His significant teachings. What Christ seems particularly to teach, as the Gospels present Him, is that the will of God is to be established by men in their human life and relationships; that God is to be served, not in meticulous restraints upon conduct, and assent to intricate theological doctrines, but in the practical conduct of life to illustrate and eventually to produce on earth the beloved community in which what the New Testament calls the kingdom of God can be revealed. No other understanding of the teaching of Christ makes intelligible His emphasis on love as the law of human relationship, so much more practical than Bergson's. It was this that New-England theology failed to comprehend and proclaim.

There is frequent discussion in some quarters about the possibility of our needing what amounts to a new religion. The Christian and historically grounded reply can be very bluntly put. We would better catch up with Him before deciding what we shall do when we have left Him behind. Whatever new religion we may discover that we need, we shall reach it only through Christ; and it can never take us beyond the revelation and character He has brought. In some way He is identical with the "God in us" of which many of these new discussions make much, and whatever it is that helps us to be our best will not be different from the light and teaching of His spirit. At one place the most liberal faith must stand in equal reverence beside the most reactionary creed. As Senator Borah said in reply to Clarence Darrow, when many years ago they were opponents in a celebrated criminal trial and Darrow had been sneering at religion: "Too late, after two thousand years, to cry 'Fraud' to the Man of Calvary! Too late, in the . . . twentieth century, to write 'impostor' on the brow of the Figure on the cross!"[12]

Even so, the eloquence of the Christian attorney does not represent the amplitude of the Christian confidence. Matthew Arnold murmuring to himself, that last day of his life, that the cross still stands, and in the straits of the soul makes its ancient appeal, carries us farther; but that, also, is still inadequate. The charter of human hope is not in the revelation of a God high and lifted up, to whom nations are but as a drop of a bucket and the small dust of the balance; but in the assurance that men are laborers together with Him. Calvary is far more than the signal flung by a rescue party to a lost expedition; it is the banner of a determined and proud advance toward a sure destination. Not alone in the straits of the soul, but in the whole march and struggle of mankind through history to the millennium, the cross, as Shelley's interrupted but greatening insight perceived, leads generations on.

References

Baillie, John, *The Place of Jesus Christ in Modern Christianity.*

Barry, Frederick R., *Christianity and the New World.*

Bergson, Henri, *The Two Sources of Morality and Religion.*

Bowie, Walter Russell, *The Renewing Gospel.*

Brightman, Edgar S., *Personality and Religion.*

Dewey, John, *A Common Faith.*

[12] Davis: *Released for Publication,* p. 41.

Grant, Frederick C., *Frontiers of Christian Thinking.*
More, Paul Elmer, *The Sceptical Approach to Religion.*
Tittle, Ernest F., *A Way of Life.*
Van Dusen, Henry P., *God in These Times.*